HATE CRIMES
WHEN INTOLERANCE TURNS VIOLENT

By Meghan Sharif

Portions of this book originally appeared in *Hate Crimes* by Michael V. Uschan.

LUCENT
P R E S S

Published in 2018 by
Lucent Press, an Imprint of Greenhaven Publishing, LLC
353 3rd Avenue
Suite 255
New York, NY 10010

Designer: Seth Hughes
Editor: Jennifer Lombardo

Cataloging-in-Publication Data

Names: Sharif, Meghan.
Title: Hate crimes: when intolerance turns violent / Meghan Sharif.
Description: New York : Lucent Press, 2018. | Series: Hot topics | Includes index.
Identifiers: ISBN 9781534561496 (library bound) | ISBN 9781534561502 (ebook)
Subjects: LCSH: Hate crimes–Juvenile literature.
Classification: LCC HV6773.5 S53 2018 | DDC 364.15–dc23

Printed in the United States of America

CPSIA compliance information: Batch #BS17KL: For further information contact Greenhaven Publishing LLC, New York, New York at 1-844-317-7404.

Please visit our website, www.greenhavenpublishing.com. For a free color catalog of all our high-quality books, call toll free 1-844-317-7404 or fax 1-844-317-7405.

CONTENTS

Adolescence is a time when many people begin to take notice of the world around them. News channels, blogs, and talk radio shows are constantly promoting one view or another; very few are unbiased. Young people also hear conflicting information from parents, friends, teachers, and acquaintances. Often, they will hear only one side of an issue or be given flawed information. People who are trying to support a particular viewpoint may cite inaccurate facts and statistics on their blogs, and news programs present many conflicting views of important issues in our society. In a world where it seems everyone has a platform to share their thoughts, it can be difficult to find unbiased, accurate information about important issues.

It is not only facts that are important. In blog posts, in comments on online videos, and on talk shows, people will share opinions that are not necessarily true or false, but can still have a strong impact. For example, many young people struggle with their body image. Seeing or hearing negative comments about particular body types online can have a huge effect on the way someone views himself or herself and may lead to depression and anxiety. Although it is important not to keep information hidden from young people under the guise of protecting them, it is equally important to offer encouragement on issues that affect their mental health.

The titles in the Hot Topics series provide readers with different viewpoints on important issues in today's society. Many of these issues, such as teen pregnancy and Internet safety, are of immediate concern to young people. This series aims to give readers factual context on these crucial topics in a way that lets them form their own opinions. The facts presented throughout also serve to empower readers to help themselves or support people they know who are struggling with many of the challenges adolescents face today. Although negative viewpoints are not ignored or downplayed, this series allows young people to see that the challenges they face are not insurmountable. Eating disorders can be overcome, the Internet can be navigated safely, and pregnant teens do not have to feel hopeless.

Quotes encompassing all viewpoints are presented and cited so readers can trace them back to their original source, verifying for themselves whether the information comes from a reputable place. Additional books and websites are listed, giving readers a starting point from which to continue their own research. Chapter questions encourage discussion, allowing young people to hear and understand their classmates' points of view as they further solidify their own. Full-color photographs and enlightening charts provide a deeper understanding of the topics at hand. All of these features augment the informative text, helping young people understand the world they live in and formulate their own opinions concerning the best way they can improve it.

Hate Crimes: An Overview

In 2015, a woman in Missoula, Montana, was charged with assaulting her neighbor during a racially-charged argument after repeatedly calling him a racial slur.

In the same year, a man in Omaha, Nebraska, stole and burnt his neighbors' gay pride flag; a swastika and the words "Hitler" and "Jews live here" were spray-painted on two houses in Rindge, New Hampshire; in a bar in Ormand Beach, Florida, a man was arrested after telling a customer that "this bar is not for blacks"[1] and hitting him with a beer bottle; and a threatening letter was left on the door of a mosque in Ames, Iowa, covered with anti-Muslim slurs and containing threats and demands that all Muslims leave the United States.

These are just a few examples of the many bias-motivated incidents that occur every day all over the United States. The people who committed these crimes were charged with various criminal offenses, including vandalism, arson, and assault. They were also charged with hate crimes.

The Definition of a Hate Crime

People began to use the term "hate crime" to refer to offenses such as these in the late 1980s following the death of 23-year-old Michael Griffith, a black man. Griffith was walking through Howard Beach, New York, on December 20, 1986, when three white people attacked him because they did not want black people in their neighborhood. After beating Griffith, the white people chased him. Griffith was so terrified and wanted to get away from his tormentors so badly that he ran onto a busy highway. He died when a car struck him.

Griffith's death and other hate-related incidents created a growing awareness about this problem and led Congress to pass the Hate Crime Statistics Act in April 1990. Annually since 1992, the Federal Bureau of Investigation (FBI) has collected and published data on hate crimes to keep law enforcement officials and the public aware of the problem. The FBI compiles the statistics with the help of state and local law enforcement officials. These statistics provide a rough idea of how many hate crimes take place in a given year, but they are not perfect. According to the Associated Press, not all state and local law enforcement agencies report hate crimes to the FBI. This means the numbers are likely much larger in reality. Experts say the FBI's numbers are not entirely reliable, but they are the best estimate the United States currently has. The Southern Poverty Law Center (SPLC) and activist Shaun King each began tracking hate-crime reports after the 2016 presidential election, but these tracking projects have not been going on long enough to provide evidence of trends.

In *Hate Crime Statistics 2015*, the FBI listed 5,818 hate-crime incidents. These crimes involved 5,493 offenders and 7,121 victims. The FBI defines hate crimes as

> *criminal offenses that are motivated, in whole or in part, by the offender's bias against [the victim]. In its broadest sense, the term refers to an attack on an individual or his or her property (e.g., vandalism, arson, assault, murder) in which the victim is intentionally selected because of his or her race, color, religion, national origin, gender, disability, or sexual orientation.*[2]

A hate crime is any criminal offense in which bias—prejudice against or hatred of an individual based on criteria such as race or sexual orientation—is the reason the perpetrator committed the act. The statistics categorize hate crimes according to the bias that motivated them. These categories include race, religion, sexual orientation (whether someone is gay, lesbian, bisexual, transgender, etc.), ethnic background or national origin, and physical or mental disabilities.

All the incidents from 2015 that were previously listed are considered hate crimes under this definition. The first and fourth victims were targeted based on race, the second based on sexual orientation, and the third and fifth for their religious beliefs.

The death of Michael Griffith changed the lives of his family. His mother and younger brother are shown here.

Evil Acts

The offenses that constitute hate crimes are endless. They range from nonviolent acts, such as spray-painting offensive graffiti on buildings, to violent acts, such as arson, assault, rape, and murder. No matter what type of conduct is involved, hate crimes are triggered by the same factor—hatred of the victims because they are different in some way from the perpetrator.

One of history's most infamous hate crimes occurred during World War II when the Nazis systematically murdered 11 million people in the Holocaust. The Nazis built death camps in which they killed many types of people whom they considered inferior because they were different: Jews, the Romani people (also known as gypsies), Slavic people from Poland and Russia, homosexuals, and people with mental or physical disabilities. Elie Wiesel, a Jew, survived Nazi death camps and wrote about his experiences during the Holocaust. He once said that hatred of people who are different is such a powerful force that it allows people to commit the worst crimes imaginable: "Hatred is at the root of evil everywhere. Racial hatred, ethnic hatred, political hatred, religious hatred. In its name, all seems permitted. For those who glorify hatred [the] end justifies all means, including the most despicable ones."[3]

CHAPTER 1

Why Do People Hate?

On June 17, 2015, nine African Americans who were attending a Bible study at a church in Charleston, South Carolina, were shot to death by 21-year-old Dylann Roof. In the investigation of this mass murder, much about Roof's motivations was revealed. He claimed that he wanted to start a race war. Before committing this terrible crime, he spent a lot of time participating in white supremacist communities online. He kept to himself, used drugs, and did not have a stable place to live, bouncing between the homes of friends and various family members before the shooting. He wrote extensively about his belief that white people were being unfairly victimized by black people, whom he believed were more likely to be criminals than white people. He believed there was a conspiracy to hide this information, and the racist groups he found online were the only ones telling the real truth. On these message boards, he found someone to blame for the difficulties he was experiencing in his life, and he found a community that supported his growing hatred.

Dylann Roof did not belong to any in-person hate groups, and he had black friends at school when he was younger. He did not start out as a violent racist. The prosecutor at his trial said that he had radicalized himself by seeking out hateful communities online and finding their biased views to be justification for his future violent plans. Even some of the hate groups that Roof idolized spoke out against his crime—the killing of innocent women and elderly people at a church meeting was too much, even for those who called for their followers to break the law in other ways.

In 2016, a federal court convicted Roof of using a firearm to commit murder, and he was also convicted of civil rights violations, including hate-crime charges. He was sentenced to death.

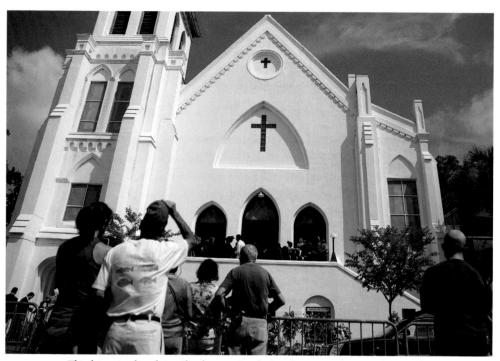

This historic church in Charleston, South Carolina, was the site of a racially motivated mass shooting in 2015 that took the lives of nine African Americans.

Are You Like Me?

When humans see or meet other people for the first time, they note facts about them such as their age, their race, how they dress, and how they speak. Sara Bullard, a sociologist and expert on how to be tolerant of other people, explained that making such comparisons is a natural part of human nature: "The first thing we do when we notice strangers is to notice the ways they are like us or different from us."[4] She stated that humans do this in an attempt to understand other people in relation to themselves. Humans generally feel more comfortable with people who are similar to them. Bullard wrote, "We gravitate toward those who are like us. We are apparently born with a tendency to prefer the familiar and withdraw from the unfamiliar."[5]

For example, when people get on a bus, they prefer to sit next to someone they know rather than a stranger. If they do not know anyone, they will generally look to share a seat with someone who is like them in some way—young or old, white or black, male or female. People prefer to sit next to someone who shares a familiar characteristic with them because it makes that person seem less like a stranger. Sociologists and psychologists claim that most people are cautious about strangers due to a fear that goes back to humankind's primitive ancestors.

FROM CHILDHOOD

"Children are socialized to hate [people who are different] in exactly the same way they are socialized to accept other conceptions of what should be valued, such as motherhood, patriotism, and personal success."
–Jack Levin and Gordana Rabrenovic, authors

Jack Levin and Gordana Rabrenovic, *Why We Hate*. Amherst, NY: Prometheus, 2004, p. 69.

In *Why We Hate*, authors Jack Levin and Gordana Rabrenovic explain that thousands of years ago, primitive people feared anyone who was not a member of their immediate group, whether that unit was a family or a tribe: "The survival of early humankind depended in part on being wary of strangers. Until and unless they were proven otherwise, outsiders were considered the enemy."[6] Levin and Rabrenovic said this fear helped primitive people survive because strangers did sometimes attack them, steal their food, seize their land, or kill them. Primitive people recognized strangers by the ways in which they were different, whether it was their physical features, language, or clothing.

Along with other psychologists and sociologists, Levin and Rabrenovic believe that most humans today still instinctively fear people who are different. They claim that this trait has been passed down to modern men and women both genetically and through learned behavior instilled in them from generation to generation. Psychologist Ervin Staub believes this fear of strangers has an important effect on human relations. He argues that mentally dividing people into two categories—those who are similar and those who are not—is a key step toward hating people who are different: "Hate is rooted in and develops from the human tendency to differentiate between *us* and *them* and the many ways that people come to devalue [think negatively about] *them*. The line between *us* and *them* can be drawn on many bases, and it can be arbitrarily and easily created."[7] The differences humans use to assign other people to such groups are almost limitless. They range from race or religion to the school the other person attends and even the sports team they like.

Throughout history, human beings have been suspicious of those they see as being different.

In Group, Out Group

When humans divide their world into "us" and "them," they no longer recognize members of "them" groups as individuals; they see them only as units of a group. This is important because humans have different methods of relating to people they have assigned to a group and people they meet and judge on an individual basis.

Hatred in the Animal Kingdom

As author Sara Bullard wrote in her book *Teaching Tolerance*, scientists believe that one of the traits humans have inherited from their animal ancestors is the tendency to reject members of their species who are different. This is true of chimpanzees, a primate closely related to humans through evolution:

Chimpanzees are famously friendly among their own groups, but they "simply can't stand the sight of strangers," observed [scientist] Carl Sagan in his book Shadows of Forgotten Ancestors. *Unfamiliar chimps provoke immediate outrage. They are routinely attacked and killed. In 1966, Jane Goodall was watching when a polio epidemic struck a group of chimps at Gombe Reservation in Tanzania, leaving several chimps partially paralyzed. Goodall wrote: "Crippled by their disease, they were forced to move in odd ways, dragging limbs. Other chimps were at first afraid; then they threatened the afflicted, and then attacked them." The insistence on the dominance of "our" group and the antagonism toward strangers is very common among animals.*[1]

1. Sara Bullard, *Teaching Tolerance: Raising Open-Minded, Empathetic Children.* New York, NY: Doubleday, 1996, p. 28.

Psychologists Robert M. Baird and Stuart E. Rosenbaum have claimed that humans generally rely on stereotypes—prejudgments of entire groups—to guide their actions toward people they consider different. Baird and Rosenbaum have stated that people like to apply stereotypes about groups to all their members because it is faster and easier than assessing each person on an individual basis: "We humans have a need to simplify our interactions with others into efficient patterns. This essential simplification leads naturally to stereotyping as a means to the desired efficiency."[8]

There are many problems with using stereotypes. One problem is that each member of any group has their own strengths and weaknesses. Additionally, stereotypes are often false because they are based on limited contact with such people; many white people who hate black people, for example, rarely have much social contact with them. The third problem is that group stereotypes are almost always negative.

Gordon W. Allport, a psychologist who pioneered key theories about hatred, claimed that people willingly accept such negative stereotypes because of a basic human need to feel superior to other people. Allport wrote, "The easiest idea to sell anyone is that he is better than someone else."[9] Thus, white people are eager to believe that they are inherently smarter than black people, people born in the United States are eager to believe that they are superior to natives of other countries, and members of any religion are eager to believe that their faith is the only true one. However, people are not born believing stereotypes and rejecting those who are different. Instead, they must learn such prejudices before they can begin hating other people.

Stereotypes are shallow oversimplifications of diverse groups of people.

Stereotypes

In their book *Hate Crimes Revisited*, sociologists Jack Levin and Jack McDevitt discussed how people learn to hate others:

Learning to hate is almost as inescapable as breathing. Like almost everyone else, the hate crime offender grows up in a culture that defines certain people as righteous, upstanding citizens, while designating others as sleazy, immoral characters who deserve to be mistreated. As a child, the perpetrator may never have had a firsthand experience with members of the groups he later comes to despise and then victimize. But, early on, merely by conversing with his family, friends, and teachers or by watching his favorite television programs, he learns the characteristics of disparaging stereotypes. He also learns that it is socially acceptable, perhaps even expected, to repeat racist jokes and use ethnic slurs and epithets. Columnist Walter Lippmann long ago coined the term "stereotype" in references to the "pictures in our heads"—the generalizations that we have concerning different groups of people. All the members of Group W are "terrorists who hate Americans." All the members of Group X are "dirty" and "lazy." All the members of Group Y are "money hungry," "powerful," and "shrewd." All the members of Group Z are "sexual predators."[1]

1. Jack Levin and Jack McDevitt, *Hate Crimes Revisited: America's War Against Those Who Are Different.* Cambridge, MA: Westview, 2002, p. 27.

Hateful Lessons

A prejudice is a preconceived negative attitude toward members of a particular group that is not based on facts. Prejudices can be learned from many sources. Three main influences on the ideas and attitudes that people acquire about their world while they are growing up, including prejudices, are their families, the culture of the community in which they live, and mass media.

A person's family is an especially powerful influence. From the day children are born, parents and other relatives teach them

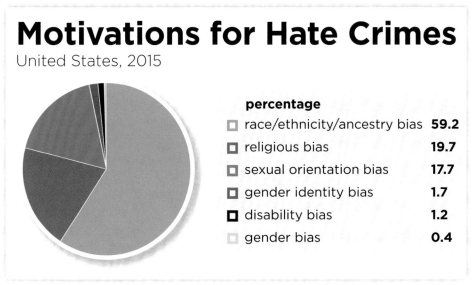

Motivations for Hate Crimes
United States, 2015

percentage

☐ race/ethnicity/ancestry bias	**59.2**
☐ religious bias	**19.7**
☐ sexual orientation bias	**17.7**
☐ gender identity bias	**1.7**
☐ disability bias	**1.2**
☐ gender bias	**0.4**

There are many different reasons why people are targeted for hate crimes, as this information from the FBI shows.

a multitude of lessons about values, priorities, and attitudes. One of the most important lessons children learn from their parents is how to act toward other people. For example, if a child's parents hate black people, that boy or girl is likely to adopt similar racist feelings. Clinton Sipes spent time in prison for hate crimes but later rejected his hatred of black people. He said his racism was shaped by his parents' attitudes: "The house I grew up in, when [civil rights leader] Martin Luther King, Jr., was mentioned on TV, it was 'There's that agitator, that problem-maker.' All I ever heard was bad things about Martin Luther King."[10] The negative comments about King that Sipes heard led him to believe that all black people were bad. This attitude led him to dislike them even before he met them.

Children can also be influenced by cultural attitudes held by the people in the community, state, and region in which they live. Children learn from comments they hear daily from friends, neighbors, and other people. If people whom children respect make negative statements about black people, LGBT+ people, or immigrants, or if they treat them with disrespect, children will tend to adopt similar attitudes toward these groups. This is especially true if the person making the negative comment is an authority figure such as a teacher, a church or community leader, or an elected official.

Gregory M. Herek is a professor of psychology at the University of California, Davis. He believes a major factor in the infamous murder of Matthew Shepard on October 6, 1998, was that so many people in Wyoming hated gay people that this hatred was culturally acceptable. After meeting Shepard in a bar in Laramie, Wyoming, Russell Henderson and Aaron McKinney robbed and beat the University of Wyoming student. They then tied Shepard to a fence and left him to die. Herek claimed the two men thought their actions were justified by antigay sentiments they had heard throughout their lives:

> The killers most certainly had a lifelong exposure to society's messages about how men and women should behave and how homosexuals should be regarded. They may have believed that no one would mind the loss of another homosexual. [Such] attacks can persist only when society defines itself in terms of "us" and "them," and systematically deprives "them" of their humanity.[11]

The mass media also shapes attitudes about people who are different. Internet articles and news reports about LGBT+, Latinx, and Muslim communities influence how people feel about them. For example, news articles about high crime levels in black neighborhoods may make readers feel that all black people are criminals, even though that is not true. Television shows and films sometimes lend believability to stereotypes by using them to shape how fictional characters are portrayed.

PLAYGROUND BULLIES

"By the time most children are big enough to ride a bicycle, they know who the outsiders are and they know what to call them: jerk, fatso, nerd ... No one had to explain these things. It's one of the inevitable lessons of being alive in America."

–Sara Bullard, sociologist

Sara Bullard, *Teaching Tolerance: Raising Open-Minded, Empathetic Children.* New York, NY: Doubleday, 1996, p. 8.

Even popular music can reinforce stereotypes. The rap group Public Enemy has been criticized for anti-Semitic, or anti-Jewish, lyrics in its songs. Richard Griffin, a group member known as Professor Griff, once used an anti-Semitic stereotype in a news conference when he claimed, "Jews are wicked. They create wickedness around the globe."[12] Likewise, other rappers have used anti-gay slurs in their lyrics. Although these and other artists have been publicly criticized for prejudicial comments and lyrics, their popularity is hardly diminished by such controversy. They have huge fan bases, so the stereotypes they spread reach listeners around the world, influencing the beliefs of devoted fans. However, such comments and song lyrics are more than mere entertainment; they are classified as hate speech. Hate speech is one of several factors that can trigger people to commit hate crimes.

Some people are taught to hate others from a young age.

When Words Become Actions

The term "hate speech" refers to any form of expression designed to hurt or belittle members of a particular group. It includes offensive comments printed on pamphlets or posters, graffiti in the form of racist slogans or symbols painted on buildings, and symbolic acts such as burning a cross—a traditional tactic used by a hate group called the Ku Klux Klan (KKK) to frighten black people and Catholics. Most hate speech is legal in the United States because the First Amendment to the U.S. Constitution guarantees freedom of speech.

During a 2001 debate in Texas regarding a hate-crime bill, state representative Senfronia Thompson, an African American, explained the dividing line that separates the two forms of hate: "You want to call me all kinds of names? … Help yourself. But the minute you hit me, you better look out, because it becomes something else."[13] Thompson knows that a punch, unlike a racial slur, is considered a hate crime.

However, hate speech is not harmless; it can encourage people to commit hate crimes. That may have been the case with Benjamin Nathaniel Smith. In 1999, Smith killed two people and wounded nine more in a three-day shooting spree motivated by his hatred of blacks, Asians, and Jews. The hate rampage ended when Smith killed himself after being surrounded by law enforcement officers. Several months earlier, Smith had explained in an interview for a documentary film how websites had helped him clarify his views toward such people. According to Smith, "It wasn't really 'til I got on the Internet, read some literature of these groups that [his hate-filled ideas] really all came together. It's a slow, gradual process to become racially conscious."[14] Reading such hateful ideas strengthened Smith's racism and compelled him to embark on a murderous rampage.

In addition to hate speech, specific events or situations can also trigger hate crimes. The September 11, 2001, terrorist attacks on the United States by the militant Islamist group al-Qaeda led to many hate crimes against Muslims. Increased tension over illegal Mexican immigration in 2005 and 2006 ignited a wave of ethnic hate crimes against Latinx, even those who were neither Mexican nor undocumented immigrants. After Donald Trump was elected president in 2016, the number of reported hate crimes against Muslims and Latinx increased, as some of Trump's supporters took his election as permission to openly express racist views. Hate-crime experts claim that most of the people who committed such offenses already hated Muslims and Latinx and were only using those events as an excuse to harm them. On May 17, 2006, Mark Potok, editor-in-chief of the SPLC's quarterly journal and *HateWatch* blog, said hate groups were using the illegal immigration issue to make people angry enough to physically assault Latinx and to deny Latinx their rights: "They're trying to generate a hostile social climate that fosters bigotry and violence towards all Hispanics, whether they're in the country illegally or not."[15]

IGNORANCE CAUSES VIOLENCE

"Hate crimes directed at individuals with disabilities are perhaps the most insidious of all unlawful behaviors. Even a single hate crime reminds us that ignorance begets [creates] negative attitudes that beget prejudice that begets hatred that begets violence."
– research team from Virginia
Commonwealth University

Brian T. McMahon et al., "Hate Crimes and Disability in America," *Rehabilitation Counseling Bulletin*, 2004, p. 768. www.academia.edu/1535991/Hate_Crimes_and_Disability_in_America.

Seen as Less Than Human

Although many people hate others for being different, very few of the haters commit hate crimes. Sociologists Jack Levin and Jack McDevitt claimed that most people who commit hate crimes have something in common: a belief that their victims are so inferior to them that they cannot be considered human beings. This belief makes perpetrators feel it is all right to do things to their victims they would never think about doing to someone they considered human, including beating and even murdering them. Levin and McDevitt wrote,

> If he [the perpetrator] views the target of his attack as a flesh-and-blood human being with feelings, friends, and a family, the offender may feel guilty. By accepting a dehumanized image of the victim, however, the perpetrator may actually come to believe that his crime was justified. After all, the rules of civilized society apply only to human beings, not to demons or animals.[16]

Hated for Their Race

In August 2011, an African American man and his white co-worker were listening to and singing along with music by an African American artist on their lunch break when Ryan Zietlow-Brown approached them. He told the white coworker that if he was really white, he should not listen to that kind of music. The two friends told him to mind his own business and walked away. A little while later, Zietlow-Brown came back. This time, he approached the African American man and stabbed him repeatedly in the head with a pair of scissors.

Zietlow-Brown was a type of white supremacist known as a skinhead. Skinheads shave their heads and typically wear jeans with suspenders and heavy boots. Although there are some anti-racist skinheads, the term is associated with racism and violence. Zietlow-Brown admitted in court that his violent attack was motivated by racism. Like neo-Nazis, skinheads are not an organized group, but there also are many white supremacist hate organizations operating in the United States, including the KKK and the American Vanguard. Hate groups vary in their methods, but they have one thing in common: They believe that white people are naturally superior to people of other races. Some believe that white people should have their own society where they live separately from other races, and others believe that all people of color should be eliminated.

Not every racially motivated hate crime is related to white supremacy, although some are. People may hold racist views without believing that all white people are inherently superior to people of color, and crimes motivated by racial bias can be carried out by people of all races, not just white people. Whenever a person is targeted for a crime because of their race, a hate crime has occurred.

Hate Group Activity in the United States, 2014

←———fewer   more———→

0   1.5   3   4.5   6

This information from the SPLC shows the number of active hate groups per 1 million residents in each state in the continental United States as of 2014.

Racist Hate Crimes

In *Hate Crime Statistics 2015*, the FBI reported that 56.9 percent of all hate crimes were motivated by racial bias. Of those 4,029 incidents, 52.7 percent were committed against blacks, 18.2 percent against whites, 9.4 percent against Latinx, 3.4 percent against American Indians or Native Americans, and 3.3 percent against Asians. Statistics alone, though, fail to convey the human toll of hate crimes. In 2003, for example, white college students attacked Jeff Woo and four Chinese friends in San Francisco, California. Woo was knocked to the ground by a punch and was then kicked repeatedly by students shouting racial slurs. Woo said he and his friends were hurt by the fact that they were attacked because of their race. "Hatred just because we're Chinese is pretty messed up,"[17] he said.

The attack on Woo was motivated by a particular form of hatred—racism. In *White Supremacy*, George Frederickson explained that for some people, the physical, cultural, and social differences they have learned to hate can be attributed to a person's race: "Racists make the claim that such differences are due mainly to immutable [unchangeable] genetic factors."[18] Throughout U.S. history, African Americans have suffered an enormous amount of racial injustice.

Organized Violence Against African Americans

In 1619, the first black people to arrive in the English colony of Virginia were slaves. For the next two centuries, African Americans were bought and sold as property. They had no rights and were whipped for minor offenses such as talking back to their white masters—brutal treatment that today would be considered a hate crime.

In the United States, slavery did not end until 1865, when the 13th Amendment to the Constitution was ratified. However, the abolition of this cruel practice did not end mistreatment of black Americans. White racists immediately began a campaign of violence to keep African Americans politically and socially powerless. Acting individually or in groups such as the KKK, whites beat, raped, and murdered blacks. Whites did this to make blacks so afraid that they would always accept whatever whites did to them. This included forcing blacks to endure segregation, which was a legal and social system that reduced blacks to second-class citizens by denying them civil rights such as the right to vote.

A favorite fear tactic whites used against blacks was lynching. This term originally meant putting a criminal to death without

*"Strange Fruit" is a haunting song about lynching in the
American South. Billie Holiday, shown here, recorded the most famous version.*

due process of law, but after the American Civil War, it became
synonymous with organized brutality against blacks. Between
1882 and 1968, when the last officially documented lynching
occurred, whites killed at least 3,445 black men, women, and
children by hanging, shooting, burning, stabbing, and torturing them. The violence continued unrestricted until the 1960s,
when federal, state, and local governments finally began protecting black people. However, even today, African Americans are
not safe from racism.

CRUEL TEASING

"At age ten [in 1985], I immigrated from China to Oakland, California … In elementary school my name soon became 'Ching Chong,' 'Chinagirl,' and 'Chow Mein.' Other children laughed at my language, my culture, my ethnicity, and my race."
–Ying Ma, author

Ying Ma, "Black Racism," *American Enterprise*, November/December 1998, p. 54.

Racism Against Black People Today

Some people continue to express racist ideas. They distribute literature and operate websites that demean blacks, record racist songs, and burn crosses—a traditional KKK symbol of racial hatred. One of the most common hate crimes against black people is to paint racist graffiti on homes and buildings. On the evening of July 8, 2006, someone spray-painted a red swastika— an infamous Nazi symbol—across the garage door of a home in Lake Elsinore, California, that was owned by Nannette Simmons, who is black. Simmons said, "If someone was trying to scare us it didn't work—we're not easily intimidated."[19] Simmons's home was also defaced with the symbol in 1995, when she first came to the predominantly white community. It is believed that black people moving into previously white neighborhoods ignite almost half of all racially-inspired hate crimes.

Racial hatred also still sparks violence. On June 7, 1998, 49-year-old James Byrd Jr. was murdered in Jasper, Texas. Byrd was chained to a pickup truck and dragged for 3 miles (4.8 km). When Jasper County sheriff Billy Rowles questioned Shawn Allen Berry, one of three white men whom witnesses claimed they had seen with Byrd the night he died, he confessed that they had attacked Byrd because he was African American. The attack on Byrd by Shawn Allen Berry, John William King, and Lawrence Russell Brewer was not motivated by an argument or disagreement between Byrd and the white men; it was not motivated by theft or any other typical reason for a crime. Berry and the other two men attacked Byrd simply because of their hatred for African Americans. Rowles was shocked at the hatred for black people that Berry expressed in his confession, which was laced with racial slurs: "That just echoed in my head. That's when we realized what we had [was a hate crime]."[20] Byrd remained alive through most of the attack, and the brutal slaying was considered one of the most vicious hate crimes that had occurred in decades.

Race was also the motivating factor in Kenosha, Wisconsin, when James Langenbach used his car to try to kill two 14-year-old black boys. The victims, Austin Hansen-Tyler and Dontrell Langston, were riding bicycles and escaped serious injury. When Kenosha County circuit judge Michael Wilk sentenced Langenbach to 176 years in prison on April 25, 2002, he lectured him on what he had done: "It was a despicable act. There are no words that adequately describe the repugnance and revulsion that a civilized person should feel. You are deserving of the contempt and scorn of a civilized society."[21]

The KKK operates in many American communities and carries out criminal intimidation targeting black families.

Looking for Excuses to Hate

During the 1980s, Chippewa groups used treaty rights they had won a century earlier to use nets to catch walleyes in northern Wisconsin lakes. White people were angry that they would not be able to catch as many fish in the same lakes and resorted to violent tactics to try to stop the Native Americans. Whites issued death threats to tribal leaders and staged protests in which they carried racist signs that read, "Save a Walleye, Spear a Pregnant Squaw." James Jannett, a tribal attorney for the Lac du Flambeau Band of Lake Superior Chippewa, testified in 1988 about the violence against the Chippewa. His testimony is excerpted from Barbara Perry and Linda Robyn's article, "Putting Anti-Indian Violence in Context":

I was out by the boat landing one night where there was over a thousand people chanting racial things. One day we were setting the nets and they were throwing rocks and they were shooting, shooting wrist rockets, slingshots with ball bearings. One hit Sarah [Jannett's daughter] in her side, and knocked her to the bottom of the boat. I got hit too. We had people chase us, we had people follow us. We had threats, we had people pushing. [They] would throw lit cigarettes at us. They would spit on us, throw rocks.[1]

1. Quoted in Barbara Perry and Linda Robyn, "Putting Anti-Indian Violence in Context: The Case of the Great Lakes Chippewas of Wisconsin," *American Indian Quarterly*, Summer 2005, p. 628.

Racism Against Native Americans

Nearly four centuries after the first black slaves were brought to the United States, acts of hatred and violence continue to plague African Americans. Native Americans, however, have suffered from racism even longer. In the 1500s, when Spanish, French, and English explorers arrived on the shores of the land that would become the United States, they were greeted by people who had already lived there for thousands of years. The languages, cultures, and physical characteristics of these

Native Americans—who are sometimes called First Americans or American Indians—all seemed strange to white Europeans. Europeans considered Native American cultures and religions inferior to European ways. Over the next three centuries, westward expansion of the United States to the Pacific Ocean came at the expense of Native Americans. White settlers and U.S. officials used their belief that they were superior to Native Americans to justify taking their homelands and confining them to reservations. Native Americans were not granted citizenship until 1924, when Congress passed the Indian Citizenship Act. The legislation was sparked by the heroic way in which thousands of Native Americans had fought for their country during World War I.

The new law, however, did not wipe out racism against Native Americans. In the early hours of June 11, 2006, three white teenagers in Farmington, New Mexico, beat up 46-year-old William Blackie, a Navajo. Reports that the trio of attackers yelled racial slurs and made remarks that demeaned Blackie's Native American heritage did not surprise 47-year-old Evan Garfield, a Navajo friend of the victim. "It [racism] is always there,"[22] Garfield said.

CALLS FOR VIOLENCE

"In 1999, 'Indian Hunting Season' flyers were distributed in South Dakota advertising an 'open season on the Sioux reservations' ... The flyers set bag limits of 10 Indians per day with a limit of 40."
–Valerie Taliman, journalist

Valerie Taliman, "Hate Crime Shocks Paiute Reservation," *Indian Country Today*, March 2, 2005, p. A1.

Although the United States is the traditional homeland of Native Americans, the group's minority status and perceived physical and cultural differences set it apart from mainstream America. Such differences are generally more apparent among immigrant populations, such as Asians.

Mistaken Identity

One of the most infamous cases of racial violence involved mistaken identity. In 1982, two white men in Detroit beat to death a Chinese man named Vincent Chin because they thought he was Japanese. They hated the Japanese because sales of Japanese automobiles had forced U.S. companies to lay off workers. In her online article for USAsians.net, Christine Ho recounted how Chin died:

"It Isn't Fair." These words were Vincent Chin's last before he lost consciousness. On June 19, 1982, Chin, a 27-year-old Chinese American, was beaten to death with a baseball bat in Detroit [by] Ronald Ebens and Michael Nitz, who blamed Japanese carmakers for Detroit's problems in the auto industry. Ebens was heard saying, "It is because of you little [expletives] that we're out of work!" [Ebens] hit Chin several times with the bat on the back and head causing Chin to fall on the ground. Fighting continued with Ebens as the aggressor. [Chin] lapsed into a severe coma, and after emergency surgery, he was pronounced brain dead. Four days later on June 23, 1982, the ventilator through which he was breathing was removed and he died.[1]

1. Christine Ho, "The Model Minority Awakened: The Murder of Vincent Chin." us_asians.tripod.com/articles-vincentchin.html.

Hate Crimes Against Asians

Like Native Americans, Asians have suffered greatly throughout U.S. history. They faced hatred from the time they first began moving to the United States in large numbers during the mid-19th century. Tens of thousands of Chinese began immigrating to the United States in 1848 after gold was discovered in California. For many decades, Chinese men and women were denied citizenship and other rights and were forced to live in segregated areas in cities. Some white people physically attacked Chinese men and women, and large groups sometimes invaded Chinatowns to burn and destroy businesses and homes.

Succeeding waves of immigrants from other Asian countries have faced similar racial hatred since then. Among the latest groups to face such animosity have been Southeast Asians from Vietnam, Laos, and Cambodia who fled to the United States after the Vietnam War ended in 1975 because they did not want to live in a Communist country. On July 14, 2001, Thung Phetakoune, a 62-year-old immigrant from Laos, was murdered in Newmarket, New Hampshire. Richard Labbe said he shot Phetakoune because "those Asians killed my brother and uncle in Vietnam. Call it payback."[23] Labbe was angry with the Asian Communists who had killed his relatives in combat. He targeted Phetakoune because his ethnicity and outward appearance matched Labbe's

Anti-Japanese sentiment during World War II can be seen in signs such as this one, which were prominently displayed in many communities to make Japanese immigrants feel unwelcome.

stereotypical image of an Asian Communist. Unfortunately, if Labbe had known anything about his victim—other than the fact that he was Southeast Asian—he would have realized that Phetakoune also hated Communists and had fled their rule in Laos.

Hatred of Asians was also a factor in a burglary in New Port Richey, Florida, on March 18, 2006. After police arrested Mark David Adge for breaking into an Asian market, they declared it was a hate crime because of the racial slurs Adge made while in custody. Adge's hatred of Asians was the motivation for the crime. Like the majority of people who commit hate crimes, Adge is white. However, blacks, Asians, and members of other racial groups who are often victims of hate crimes also have prejudices, and they, too, sometimes commit hate crimes.

Racial Hatred by People of Color

On June 5, 2006, while Kim McCandless was trying to find a parking spot in the Sunrise Mall in Massapequa, New York, Carl Graves threw a chunk of cement at her vehicle. The 20-year-old black man acted because he was angry that white people were shopping at his neighborhood mall. McCandless was upset that the four small children with her could have been hurt. She was even angrier when she learned why she was attacked: "To know it's about a skin color bothers me even more."[24] Graves was charged with a hate crime.

Some black people attack white people to seek vengeance for white racism. On October 7, 1989, in Kenosha, Wisconsin, a group of black men watched *Mississippi Burning*, a film about white racists killing a black civil rights worker. Afterward, when they saw a 14-year-old white boy walking down the street, 19-year-old Todd Mitchell asked the other men, "Do you all feel hyped up to move on some white people?"[25] The black men decided to take out their anger over what they had seen in the movie on the white boy. They beat him severely and stole his sneakers.

Blacks and Latinx sometimes commit hate crimes against each other. In Los Angeles, California, four members of a Latinx gang were charged with a hate crime for murdering

Kenneth Wilson. On June 27, 2006, assistant U.S. attorney Alex Bustamante said during their trial that they killed Wilson "because he was black [and] gang members had promised each other, had agreed that they would drive African Americans out of the neighborhood, by threats, by force, by murder."[26] Bustamante said the murder was part of a six-year gang effort to keep black people from moving to their neighborhood. All four defendants were convicted.

The Cost of Racist Hate Crimes

Columbia University law professor Kent Greenawalt stated that hate crimes not only harm the victim but also other people of the same race by frightening, humiliating, or intimidating them. Wilson's murder was a warning to all black people that they were not welcome and would not be safe in the neighborhood the Latinx gang had claimed as its own. Cross burnings are an example of a hate crime that affects an entire racial group. In an opinion defending a Virginia law that outlaws cross burnings, U.S. Supreme Court justice Clarence Thomas, an African American, declared, "There is no other purpose to the [burning] cross—no communication, no particular message. It was intended to cause fear and to terrorize a population."[27] Such acts also divide communities by increasing tensions among all white and black residents.

The greatest harm that hate crimes cause, however, is to victims and their families. When Jeff Woo and his friends were attacked because they were Chinese, the assault made Asians

AN OFFENDER'S WORDS

"I said to myself, 'The first person that I see in this mall that looks white, I'm killing.' I had never seen this woman before and I didn't care. All I knew was she had blond hair and blue eyes and she had to die."
—Phillip Grant, a black man found guilty of killing Concetta Russo-Carriero

Quoted in Anahad O'Connor, "Homeless Man Is Convicted of Murder as a Hate Crime," *New York Times*, July 12, 2006, p. B5.

fearful of the area in which the attack occurred. It also saddened them because the incident showed how much some people hated them. "We'll never forget," Woo said. "It's still inside us."[28]

A similar sense of fear existed after the 1999 shooting spree by Benjamin Nathaniel Smith, a racist who hated blacks. Ricky Byrdsong was one of the victims shot to death by Smith. Byrdsong's widow, Sherialyn, remembered how hard it was to tell her three children that their father was dead and to dis-

Hate crimes can harm an entire community—not just the victims—by creating fear.

close the manner in which he was killed. Byrdsong said, "I will never forget the look on their faces and their screams of horror and disbelief."[29]

Sometimes people who commit hate crimes regret their actions when they realize there are consequences. On June 23, 2006, Abel Castaneda was sentenced to 10 years in prison for beating up Steve Lawson. Castaneda attacked Lawson in Santa Ana, California, for one reason: Lawson is black. When Castaneda was sentenced, he told Lawson, "I'm sorry for what happened. Now we are both paying the price."[30]

Innocent Victims

Although hate-crime perpetrators such as Castaneda have earned their punishment by breaking the law, their targets are innocent victims who have done nothing to merit such abuse. After James Langenbach was sentenced to 176 years in prison, Roechita Tyler said she could not understand why Langenbach had tried to harm her son just because he was black. "Because no one deserves this. No one deserves this,"[31] she said.

CHAPTER 3

Hated for Their Religion

In 2017, a Muslim family living in Fairfax, Virginia, came home from a weekend vacation to find their home had been vandalized and some of their possessions stolen. The burglars had scrawled a crude anti-Muslim message on the living room wall, broken framed religious texts, and torn apart the family's copy of the Koran. The concerned parents sent their small children to stay with a relative because they did not want them to see the hateful message on the wall. They said they were particularly affected by the perpetrators' desecration of their sacred text. They said they considered moving, as they felt so devastated and unwelcome.

Hate crimes against Muslims increased by nearly 67 percent in 2015, perhaps in response to well-publicized attacks by Muslim terrorist groups around the world. Islam is not the only religion that is the target of biased attacks, however. Christians, Jews, and members of other religions are also targets of hate crimes.

OPPOSING INTOLERANCE

"I want to understand this to find out why we are seeing more intolerance in our society, in this particular case directed at a particular community. We can't get along in this country unless we have mutual respect and tolerance for each other."
—Senator Bill Nelson, commenting on an increase in hate crimes against Jews

Quoted in George Bennett, "Nelson Pushing Broader Federal Hate Crime Law," *Palm Beach Post*, April 12, 2006, p. B3.

Where Does Religious Hatred Come From?

One of the most important themes in Christianity, Judaism, and Islam, as well as other religions, is that people should love and respect each other. However, psychologist Ervin Staub argues that despite that central message, religious beliefs often divide people and cause some of them to hate those who follow other religions. According to Staub, "Religions, which proclaim love but at the same time almost always identify other religions as false and as the wrong way to worship God, have been both a frequent basis of differentiating *us* and *them* and a source of hate for those of other faiths."[32] For thousands of years, members of the world's three major religions—Christianity, Judaism, and Islam—have, at times, hated and warred against each other because they believe their concept of God is the only true one. Individual religions have also been divided over the proper way to worship the same God. Roman Catholicism and Protestantism are both Christian religions, but their members have often clashed because of differences in some of their beliefs and traditional ways of worship.

This popular symbol speaks out against religious bias by combining sacred symbols of multiple religious faiths in a message of unity.

Followers of Jewish, Christian, and Muslim religions brought those ancient hatreds with them when they immigrated to the United States—a fact that is reflected in statistics on U.S. religious hate crimes. In *Hate Crime Statistics 2015*, the FBI reported 1,354 criminal offenses that were motivated by religious bias. Of these offenses, 51.3 percent targeted Jews, 22.2 percent targeted Muslims, 4.4 percent targeted Catholics, 3.5 percent targeted Protestants, and the rest targeted people of various religions, including Hinduism and Buddhism. Most of those 21st-century crimes were similar to hateful acts that members of various religions have committed against each other for centuries. The religious bias that is responsible for more of these acts than any other is anti-Semitism.

Anti-Semitism

On March 4, 2006, unknown vandals painted 11 large swastikas on the Striar Jewish Community Center in Stoughton, Massachusetts. The swastika, the best-known symbol of Nazi Germany, is a bitter reminder to Jews of the Holocaust, when the Nazis murdered 11 million people, including 6 million Jews, during World War II, which lasted from 1939 to 1945. Defacing homes, synagogues, and other buildings with swastikas is one of the most common hate crimes against Jews. Such acts continue a centuries-old pattern of anti-Semitism in the United States.

Jewish people did not begin immigrating to the United States in large numbers until the late 19th century. Although even

THE FREE EXERCISE OF RELIGION

"We live in a pluralistic society where the free exercise of religion is one of the central tenets of our society. When a population within that American fabric feels targeted based solely on their religious beliefs, we believe that to be not only illegal but also un-American."
–Arsalan Iftikhar, former legal director for the Council on American-Islamic Relations

Quoted in David Hency, "Prosecutors Have Options in Mosque Case," *Portland (ME) Press Herald*, July 12, 2006, p. B1.

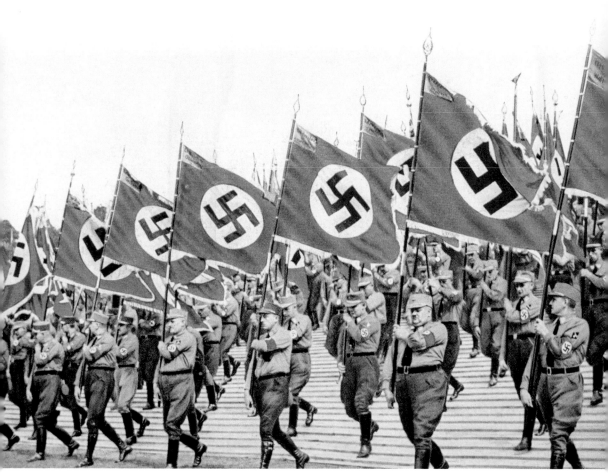

The swastika is one of the best-known symbols of Nazi Germany and is still used by hate groups in the United States today.

the few who arrived earlier had met with some hostility, anti-Semitism increased and grew stronger as the number of Jewish immigrants grew. This hatred resulted in employment and social discrimination against Jews, who also became targets of violence that today would be considered hate crimes. Anti-Semites, including members of the KKK, beat up or murdered Jewish people and burned down synagogues. Today, KKK groups continue to target Jews for hate crimes, as do neo-Nazi groups that promote German leader Adolf Hitler's racial and religious ideas that led to the Holocaust.

Christians have committed most of the hate crimes against Jews. The traditional basis for Christian anti-Semitism is the belief that Jews were responsible for killing Jesus Christ, even though it was a Roman official who ordered his death and Roman soldiers who crucified him. In 2004, actor Mel Gibson was accused of anti-Semitism for promoting this claim in his controversial film *The Passion of the Christ*. Gibson denied at the time that he hated Jews, but an incident two years later raised new questions about his beliefs. On July 28, 2006, Los Angeles County sheriff's deputy James Mee arrested Gibson for speeding and drunk driving. In his official report, Mee wrote that Gibson threatened him, "blurted out a barrage of anti-Semitic remarks about [profanity deleted] Jews," and claimed "the Jews are responsible for all the wars in the world." Gibson then asked Mee, "Are you a Jew?"[33] Gibson was so hostile that Mee requested help from other officers to arrest him.

During the late 20th century, increased immigration by Muslims brought more anti-Semitic people to the United States. Islam, like Judaism, began in the Middle East, and for centuries, members of the two religions have fought bitterly over which religion is the true one. This hatred gained strength in the early 21st century as the Jewish nation of Israel and the Muslim countries that surround it continued to clash. Anger over that situation led a few Muslims living in the United States to vandalize synagogues and attack Jews.

One of these instances occurred on July 28, 2006, when Naveed Afzal Haq killed one woman and wounded five others in a shooting rampage at the Jewish Federation of Greater Seattle in Washington. After Haq had taken people at the center hostage, he called an emergency 911 dispatcher. Haq said he hated Jews because Muslims were dying in Israel's battles with its neighbors and in the Iraq War. Although the war was waged by the United States and its allies, Haq blamed Jews for the fighting. He told the operator, "These are Jews, and I'm tired of … our people getting pushed around by the situation in the Middle East."[34]

The Legacy of 9/11

According to sociologists Jack Levin and Jack McDevitt, "On September 11, 2001, Americans witnessed the most violent single incident of hate-motivated violence in this country's history."[1] They were referring to the attack by the Muslim terrorist group al-Qaeda. They also claimed that the attack showed how one incident could create a climate that would foster thousands of hate crimes:

If we were ever unsure, the September 11 attack on America provided indisputable evidence that a single situation can precipitate major changes in the ways that we behave toward the groups in our midst. In the aftermath of the devastation created by Middle Eastern terrorists, Americans of Arab descent or Islamic religious beliefs who had previously lived in relative peace and tranquillity abruptly found themselves at great personal risk. Prejudiced feelings and beliefs about Arabs and Muslims, long hidden from view, suddenly were expressed in a generalized suspicion of anyone of Middle Eastern heritage. This suspicion was played out in violent acts across the country ranging from simple assault to murder.[2]

1. Jack Levin and Jack McDevitt, *Hate Crimes Revisited: America's War Against Those Who Are Different.* Cambridge, MA: Westview, 2002, p. 3.
2. Levin and McDevitt, *Hate Crimes Revisited*, p. 3.

Hostility Against Islam

The war in Iraq, which helped incite Haq's shooting spree, was one reason for many hate crimes against American Muslims. When al-Qaeda attacked the United States on September 11, 2001, the country's estimated 6 million American Muslims became targets for people who were angry at the Muslim terrorist group. In the first month after the attacks, more than 300 hate crimes against Muslims occurred in 38 states. By the end of 2001, the number of such offenses had nearly tripled. People shouted slurs at Muslims; made telephoned death threats;

vandalized and set fire to Muslim mosques, homes, and businesses; and beat up Muslims. In several incidents, American Muslims were even murdered. These incidents happened despite the fact that American Muslims had condemned the attack, which had killed Muslims, as well as members of other religions.

Although the pace of hate crimes against Muslims slowed after 2001, Muslims continued to be targeted for the next several years. Anti-Muslim feeling remained high in the United States because of the nation's continuing war against al-Qaeda and other Muslim terrorist groups, which included invasions of Afghanistan and Iraq. Combat deaths of U.S. soldiers in those two countries were a major source of Muslim hatred, even though many American Muslims also fought and died for their country during those wars. During the 2016 presidential election campaign season, hate crimes against Muslims rose again. According to the *New York Times*, "Some scholars believe that the violent backlash against American Muslims is driven not only by the string of terrorist attacks that began early last year, but also by the political vitriol from candidates like Donald J. Trump, who has called for a ban on immigration by Muslims and a national registry of Muslims in the United States."[35]

People who express anti-Muslim hatred often claim to be motivated by terrorism. These people overlook the fact that the majority of Muslims are not terrorists.

In the first few years of the 21st century, hatred against Muslims in the United States and other countries grew so strong that a term was coined to describe it—Islamophobia. On December 7, 2004, the United Nations (UN) met to discuss how to ease such fear and hatred. Muslim journalist Mouin Rabbani attended the UN seminar and admitted that the September 11 attack had greatly strengthened anti-Muslim feelings that had already existed. He said at the time, "My impression is that hostility to Islam as a religion has grown exponentially. A main effect of 9-11 has been to make [hatred of Muslims] not only more widespread but also considerably more mainstream and respectable—it has let the genie out of the bottle."[36]

Anti-Muslim Hate Crimes

Many of the crimes this hatred has generated have been directly against Islam. Thousands of mosques in the United States became the main targets of people who hated Muslims. During the first few years after September 11, 2001, dozens of these places of worship were vandalized with graffiti or damaged by arson fires and bombs; in Florida, one man smashed his truck into the Islamic Center of Tallahassee. In April 2006, shots were fired into a Maryland mosque, and in June 2006, a sign that claimed "Muslims Worship Satan" was left near an Arizona mosque.

Another way to attack Islam is to desecrate the Koran, the Muslim holy book. People have burned the Koran or have spit on it in public displays of hate. In July 2006, a copy of the Koran that had been riddled with bullets was tossed onto the steps of the Islamic Center of Chattanooga, Tennessee. The perpetrator also posted a video on the Internet that showed the book being struck by bullets. On July 10, 2006, Arsalan Iftikhar, who was the legal director of the Council on American-Islamic Relations at the time, condemned the incident. He claimed it was not only a hate crime but also a violation of the Muslims' right to freedom of religion. According to Iftikhar, "By throwing the bullet-riddled Quran [Koran] at the mosque, we believe the perpetrators went beyond the limits of free speech by taking part in an overt act of religious intimidation."[37]

Anti-Catholic Hate Crimes

The United States is a predominantly Christian nation, and Christians have committed most of the hate crimes against Jews and Muslims. However, one Christian group has been targeted by other Christians—Roman Catholics. Catholics have faced religious discrimination and hate crimes since the 1600s, when they first began immigrating to the English colonies that would one day become the United States. Most hatred has come from Protestants, who are members of a separate branch of Christianity who disagree with some Catholic beliefs and forms of worship. Protestants dominated the colonies, and at times, they barred Catholics from practicing their faith. When large numbers of Irish and other European Catholics began immigrating to the United States during the 19th century, Protestants used their economic and political power to discriminate against Catholics in jobs and housing. Protestant gangs also attacked Catholics and their churches, sometimes destroying the churches.

CATHOLIC CROSS BURNING

"I think it's despicable, sad, and terrible. It's such a bad thing. It really troubles me. We need to get to the bottom of it. It seems a very heinous crime."
–Rocco J. Longo, former town manager in Duxbury, Massachusetts, about a wooden cross that was set on fire at Holy Family Catholic Church

Quoted in David Abel, "Burning of Cross Probed as Hate Crime," *Boston Globe*, February 22, 2005, p. B2.

This hatred eased in the 20th century, and in 1960, John F. Kennedy overcame this prejudice to be elected the first Catholic U.S. president. However, anti-Catholic incidents sometimes still occur, such as the one that happened on June 6, 2006, at Holy Hill, a Catholic shrine near Milwaukee, Wisconsin. Two men, who were later arrested, spray-painted "Hell Will Rule" and "I'm Glad They Killed Jesus" on religious statues. During a religious service several days later at Holy Hill, Milwaukee archbishop Timothy Dolan told more than 750 people that the "gross acts of desecration" were a reminder that hatred and evil still exist. "We trust that the invincible power of Christ will reclaim this sanctuary from the forces of evil,"[38] Dolan said.

Attacks against places of worship are especially hurtful to religious communities.

A new source of Catholic hatred arose in the 1990s when many priests were charged with sexually assaulting young boys, typically in incidents that had occurred decades before. In the years since then, some hate crimes aimed at the Catholic Church have been linked to outrage over this sexual misconduct. In November 2002, someone in Everett, Massachusetts, defaced a statue and spray-painted profanity and the word "lies" on the front doors of Our Lady of Grace Catholic Church, where a former pastor had been accused of sexually molesting children. Donna Morrissey, a church spokeswoman, said even though the former pastor's actions made people angry, "I would condemn any kind of desecration of a house of worship or a statue or an incident such as this."[39]

John F. Kennedy was the first Catholic president, but his election did not eliminate prejudice against Catholics.

Hatred Against Smaller Religions

Although most religious hate crimes involve the three major religions—Christianity, Judaism, and Islam—attacks on smaller religious groups also occur. On April 5, 2006, vandals struck a Hindu temple that was under construction in the Minneapolis suburb of Maple Grove, Minnesota. The attack resulted in damages totaling $200,000 and included the destruction of important statues depicting religious deities. The vandalism forced postponement of the opening of the temple for several months, affecting the more than 20,000 Hindus in Minnesota, North Dakota, South Dakota, and Iowa who wanted to pray in the new temple. "It is an enormous tragedy. Nobody expects such things in a tolerant state like Minnesota,"[40] said former Minnesota state senator Satveer Chaudhury, a Hindu.

Anti-Amish Hatred

The Amish are Christians who are targeted for hate crimes because their religion makes them shun modern conveniences such as telephones, electricity, and automobiles. The Amish live in many rural areas in the United States. Their simple life makes them seem strange to other people, who sometimes shoot at their horse-drawn buggies. In January 2006, two teenagers in Taylor County, Wisconsin, shot paintball guns at Amish homes, damaged mailboxes, and heaved a cement block through the window of an Amish furniture store. They were charged with criminal damage to property and disorderly conduct as hate crimes. When 19-year-old Cody J. Bunkelman was arrested, he apologized but tried to minimize his actions by saying, "A lot of people mess around with the Amish."[1] Taylor County district attorney Karl Kelz responded to the crimes by saying they were something that could not be tolerated. He was quoted in Luke Klink's article for the *Milwaukee Journal Sentinel* as saying, "I am bothered by a kid who said, 'Let's go pick on the Amish.' You might as well strike out the word Amish and insert blacks, Jews, Muslims or Catholics. Rural Wisconsin can't afford to have us say, 'Don't worry about it.' That is not a good message to send."[2]

1. Quoted in Luke Klink, "Teens Accused of Targeting Amish," *Milwaukee Journal Sentinel*, January 5, 2006, p. 3B.
2. Quoted in Klink, "Teens Accused of Targeting Amish."

Such hate crimes do more harm than merely damaging places of worship. They also create mental and emotional anguish for the members of that religion. After vandals threw bricks through four windows at the Metropolitan Baptist Church in Altadena, California, in March 2006, Earl Perry, the chairman of the church's board of trustees, was upset that any person would defile a place of worship. Perry said, "It's disturbing that anyone would attack a church, to me. I was brought up to believe that the ground where a church is, is sacred, and it's hands off. I guess I'm a little old-fashioned in that."[41]

CHAPTER 4

Hated for Their
Sexual Orientation or Gender Identity

On June 12, 2016, the deadliest mass shooting in U.S. history to date took place in a gay nightclub in Orlando, Florida. While the shooter's motives were complex and not entirely clear, and may have included racist and religious biases, the Pulse nightclub shooting was classified as a hate crime against LGBT+ people. Forty-nine people were killed, many of them members of the LGBT+ community. The shooter, Omar Mateen, claimed to be a member of the militant Islamist terrorist organization ISIS, although he was not directly connected to the group in any way. Instead, it seems he learned their hateful ideology through the Internet and carried out the attack on his own. He was killed after barricading himself in a bathroom during the attack.

This horrible attack may be the worst example of violence against American LGBT+ individuals in the country's history, but it is far from the only one. Anti-LGBT+ violence is extremely common, and many members of this community are the victims of hate crimes each year. While acceptance and understanding has grown throughout the 21st century, prejudice still exists.

As is the case with other hate crimes, people who are targeted for their sexual orientation or gender identity are targeted for being seen as different. Because of who they love or how they live, they may face hatred and even violence.

The Pulse nightclub shooting remains the deadliest mass shooting in U.S. history as of 2017, and it was also a hate crime.

The Numbers

The transgender community unfortunately experiences some of the most brutal murders associated with any category of hate crimes. However, these sensational homicides are only a small percentage of the total number of offenses caused by hatred of a person's sexual preference or gender identity. In *Hate Crime Statistics 2015*, the FBI lists 1,219 incidents relating to sexual orientation and 118 related to gender identity.

Gregory M. Herek, a psychology professor at the University of California, Davis, is an expert on sexual-orientation hate crimes. He believes federal statistics paint a flawed portrait of the frequency of such offenses because many victims never report them to officials. Herek wrote, "Estimates of nonreporting among gay and lesbian hate crime victims [in various studies] have ranged as high as 90 percent."[42] Herek said that many victims do not report crimes because they believe law enforcement officials will discriminate against or mistreat them—a fear that is based on past incidents in which this has sometimes happened. Many victims also fear that they will suffer negative consequences from employers, friends, or even spouses if their sexual orientation is publicly revealed in a criminal complaint.

The Most Commonly Targeted Group

Members of the LGBT+ community live daily with the threat of violence from people who hate them. According to the *New York Times*, the LGBT+ community is the group that is most likely to be targeted for hate crimes. The National Coalition of Anti-Violence Programs (NCAVP) explained that sexual-orientation violence takes many forms—from bullying in school to rape, sexual assault, and murder. The NCAVP stated that there is so much hatred based on sexual orientation that almost every LGBT+ individual will feel the effects of a hate crime or hate incident:

The best available research suggests that 40 percent of lesbians and gay men in the U.S. consider themselves the victims of hate violence in their adult lifetimes, and that hate violence is a near-universal experience of openly LGBT youth ... [Even] the minority of LGBT people who do not personally experience [hate crimes] or other characteristic forms of violence (which include sexual assaults and abuse, "pick-up" crimes, family abuse and police misconduct) may suffer the secondary effects, when friends or family members are targeted or when they limit their own freedom or self-expression because they fear becoming victims themselves.[1]

1. "What Does NCAVP Do?," National Coalition of Anti-Violence Programs. www.ncavp.org/about/default.aspx.

Another reason why such hate crimes are underreported is because law enforcement officials and the justice system often do not categorize them as such offenses. The brutal October 2002 slaying of Gwen Araujo in Newark, California, is an example of this. Araujo, a 17-year-old transgender woman, was kicked and beaten with an iron skillet, struck with a shovel, and choked with a rope. On September 12, 2005, a jury convicted two men of second-degree murder in Araujo's death but found them innocent of hate-crime charges. Thom Lynch, executive director of the San Francisco Lesbian, Gay, Bisexual, and Transgender Community Center at the time of the verdict, criticized the jury's decision: "Only some justice has been done. The idea that hate was not a factor [in Araujo's death] is just unimaginable."[43] Because the two men had sex with Araujo, the jury decided the murder was motivated by their anger over their feeling that Araujo was biologically a man and not by a hatred of transgender people.

NO MATTER WHO YOU ARE

"Whether you're a prostitute, a bus driver, a retired U.S. Capitol police officer—all of whom I know as transgendered people—you don't deserve to be the victim of a crime."
—Brett Parson, police officer

Quoted in "D.C. Police Sgt. Brett Parson Discusses Transgender Killings," *Intelligence Report*, Winter 2003. www.splcenter.org/fighting-hate/intelligence-report/2003/dc-police-sgt-brett-parson-discusses-trangender-killings.

Despite whether such offenses are officially considered hate crimes, hatred of people for their sexual orientation is widespread, and members of the LGBT+ community must deal with this hate every day of their lives.

Anti-LGBT+ Hatred at School

School is the first place in which many people are exposed to hatred because they are different. This is especially true for LGBT+ people, who are often cruelly mocked or physically abused because of their sexual orientation or gender identity. According to a 2012 study by the Gay, Lesbian, and Straight

Education Network (GLSEN), "45 percent of teachers and 49 percent of students in elementary schools hear the term 'gay' used in a negative way by other students, making it one of the most commonly heard examples of biased language. Additionally, 26 percent of students and teachers report hearing students use outright homophobic slurs."[44]

A Survivor's Account

In a 2002 study of hate crimes based on sexual orientation, one gay man explained how he was beaten and his friend was killed when they were attacked by six men outside a bar in an unnamed southern town. The two victims were walking to their car in the bar's parking lot with two friends when six men began calling them offensive names and then started beating them. The survivor explained what happened:

My friend was hit in the head with a brick, and when he went down, they hit him more in the head with bricks and clubs till he stopped moving. I was hit in the legs with a club, and broke my knee cap. The other two friends got away and went back into the bar to call the police, and came out with more people from the bar, and chased the attackers away until the police got there. The police took about 20 minutes to get there and the ambulance almost a half an hour. By that time [my friend] had already expired. He died in my arms.[1]

1. Quoted in Gregory M. Herek, Jeanine C. Cogan, and J. Roy Gillis, "Victim Experiences in Hate Crimes Based on Sexual Orientation," *Journal of Social Issues*, 2002, vol. 58, p. 329.

LGBT+ students are also targets of hate when they attend colleges and universities. Many of the hateful acts directed against them occur in dormitories that they share with heterosexual students. One such incident occurred in Madison, Wisconsin. While yelling, "All [derogatory name for gay people] should die," four students ripped down posters that were taped to a gay University of Wisconsin student's door. The men also spit on the door and wrote on it, "I hate [derogatory name for gay people]. Die."[45] In January 2006, the four students were charged with disorderly conduct and criminal damage to property as hate crimes.

FEAR AND ISOLATION

"Hate crimes are message crimes, and the message is: You and your kind don't belong here. They are intended to create fear and isolation."
–Brian Blanchard, Dane County district attorney

Quoted in Anita Clark, "Marriage Bill Debate Stirs Fears," *Wisconsin State Journal*, April 24, 2006, p. B1.

Anti-LGBT+ Hatred in the Community

Unfortunately, LGBT+ students do not leave behind such hatred when they graduate. It follows them the rest of their lives. Heyward Drummond knows this all too well. When Drummond, who lives in Aldie, Virginia, went to get his newspaper on the morning of July 29, 2006, he saw that vandals had written an offensive term for gay people on his driveway, mailbox, and a nearby fence. They had also poured gasoline on his lawn and destroyed flowers and trees. "I just don't understand how someone could hate like that,"[46] Drummond said. However, Drummond did understand that the reason for the destruction was that someone hated the fact that he and his domestic partner, John Ellis, lived in the upscale neighborhood.

Being attacked at home makes people feel especially vulnerable because home is where most people expect to feel safest. However, a 2002 study on sexual-orientation hate crimes published in the *Journal of Social Issues* showed that LGBT+ people fear being attacked anywhere and at any time. One example the study cited was a woman and some friends who went to a public park and were beaten by three men because they were lesbians. The woman explained what happened:

> When [a friend] said she didn't want to fight, he … broke her nose. As he was getting ready to throw the punch he said "[an offensive name for lesbians]." One person [got] a cut open on their face. And another one had her collarbone broken and got knocked unconscious. I got kicked in the knee and upper thigh and was severely bruised. And then somebody came by and helped scare them away.[47]

Although many hate crimes are the result of such chance encounters, predators sometimes seek out LGBT+ individuals in what is known as "gay bashing." This happened on February 2, 2006, when Jacob Robida, age 18, went to Puzzles Lounge, a gay bar in New Bedford, Massachusetts. In a savage attack, Robida wounded two men with a hatchet and shot a third man before fleeing the establishment; the three men later recovered from their injuries. A bartender described the attack: "He started swinging the hatchet on top of this customer's head. He just had a stone-cold look on his face ... just emotionless."[48] Two days later, Robida killed himself and a companion after police stopped their car in Arkansas. The shootout ended a manhunt for Robida that had swept through several states.

Anti-Transgender Violence

Although many groups experience hate-crime vandalism and violence, it is believed that hate-related murder rates are highest for victims belonging to the LGBT+ community. None are attacked as often or as savagely as the transgender community. In a story about violence against transgender individuals, the *Intelligence Report* noted that in 2002, the FBI reported 11 hate-crime murders motivated by racial, religious, or sexual-orientation bias. In contrast, the magazine said a study it conducted based on news accounts, police reports, and other sources had documented at least 14 murders of transgender people in that same year. The discrepancy was due to federal officials attributing some of the murders to motives other than hatred over sexual orientation and gender identity.

In August 2003, two transgender women were shot and killed and several others were attacked in Washington, D.C. Jessica Xavier, a transgender activist in the nation's capital, claimed then that violence against transgender people had reached an all-time high in Washington, D.C.: "What we're seeing is a war against transgendered women. We are regarded by most as disposable people."[49] To support her claim, Xavier cited results of a study she conducted in 2000. Of 4,000 transgender people who were interviewed, 17 percent said they had been assaulted with a weapon because of their gender identity.

Each year on the Transgender Day of Remembrance, vigils are held to commemorate those who have been murdered because of their gender identity and to draw attention to the issue of violence against transgender people.

Most transgender hate crimes involve transgender women. However, one of the most infamous transgender hate crimes involved a transgender man. On December 31, 1993, Brandon Teena, Lisa Lambert, and Philip De Vine were shot and stabbed to death in rural Falls City, Nebraska. Brandon Teena was dating Lambert when John Lotter and Marvin Thomas Nissen discovered that he was transgender. They were so angry that, as they saw it, a woman was posing as a man that they raped him. After Brandon Teena reported the rape to police, the men killed him and his two friends.

MOCKED AT SCHOOL

"I guess I always kind of knew that I was a lesbian. At school, people would make fun of me [and] it got to me after a while. I feel very self-conscious about that."
—A Santa Fe, New Mexico, teenager talking about being bullied

Quoted in Teresa Baca, "Monologues Give Insight to Teens Who Are 'Out,'" *Santa Fe New Mexican*, June 9, 2006, p. D3.

The brutal incident received widespread media coverage. Gwen Smith, whose website, Remembering Our Dead, tracks anti-transgender violence, said that Brandon Teena's death helped raise awareness of such hate crimes and spurred action to stop them. Smith recalled, "It was very shocking and it was a wake-up call. After it happened the transgender community began to get together and start working on things."[50] The 1999 movie *Boys Don't Cry*, starring Hilary Swank as Brandon Teena, also helped publicize anti-transgender violence.

Brandon Teena, a transgender man, was a victim of rape and murder because of his gender identity. Actress Hilary Swank (center) played him in a movie about his life and death.

Extreme Brutality

Violent attacks such as the one that led to Teena's death are more common against members of the LGBT+ community than they are against any other group targeted by hate crimes. The extreme brutality that often accompanies these assaults causes many LGBT+ people to live in constant fear. Sara Henriksen was harassed while attending Waterloo High School in Iowa because she was a lesbian. After she was beaten up, Henriksen constantly worried about being attacked again. During a March 1, 2006, conference on gay hate crimes in Iowa, the Waterloo senior admitted that she was afraid while attending school: "I wonder if the footsteps in the hall are those of the [next] person who'll hurt me."[51] Her concern was heightened by hateful notes that fellow students stuffed in her locker.

The possibility that they will be murdered—the ultimate act of violence—is something LGBT+ people sadly understand. In June 2006, a pickup truck bearing a sign that declared LGBT+ people should all be killed was seen driving through the streets of Fort Collins, Colorado. Most people never have to worry about such threats, but some men and women in Fort Collins were afraid they would be singled out because of their sexual orientation. Diana Wess, a gay-rights spokeswoman, wrote to the *Coloradoan* newspaper to condemn the hateful act. In her letter, Wess asked readers to "imagine yourself as the target of this threatening message."[52]

Not a Choice

Wess's letter helped people understand how hateful messages hurt and upset LGBT+ people. In a similar manner, a Michigan judge tried to make a man convicted of murdering a gay man realize how terrible his crime had been. On August 8, 2006, Wayne County circuit judge David Allen sentenced 17-year-old Steven Williams Jr. of Detroit, Michigan, to 12 years in prison for shooting 31-year-old Salvagio Vonatti of Windsor, Ontario. In December 2005, Williams had shot Vonatti in the head outside of a Detroit gay bar. When Allen sentenced Williams for assault with intent to do great bodily harm and for using a firearm to commit a felony, Vonatti was still in a coma and was not expected to recover. Calling the attack an anti-gay hate crime, Allen told Williams that the things he and the victim had in common were greater than their differences:

> Like you [Vonatti] is a son, brother, uncle, cousin, friend and lover. He loved and was loved and was on this earth to be left alone in peace and happiness. Who and how he loved was none of your business and was no threat to you and the community. Let's also get one other thing straight that came up in trial. Homosexuality is not a "lifestyle" or "choice." Homosexuality is no different than the color of your eyes or hair. [Would] anyone in their right mind choose to be homosexual with predators like you shooting them in the head for being gay?[53]

Hated for Being Different

In December 2016, four black teenagers from Chicago, Illinois, filmed themselves torturing an 18-year-old white man with schizophrenia and attention deficit disorder (ADD). During the attack, the assailants forced the victim to make statements related to race. However, the crime was believed to be motivated not by racism, but by hatred against those with disabilities. The young man was beaten, robbed, cut with a knife, and humiliated by being forced to drink toilet water. This brutal assault was posted on Facebook by the perpetrators as a way of bragging about their crime. This video led to their arrest, after which they were all charged with kidnapping, assault, and hate crimes.

This incident is one of many perpetrated against those with disabilities in the United States. People with physical, mental, or intellectual disabilities are often targeted by those who hate them for being different. In addition to people with disabilities, people who are perceived as different because of their national origin or the fact that they are homeless are also the targets of hate crimes.

Hated for Where They Come From

The FBI's annual *Hate Crime Statistics* report lists crimes motivated by xenophobia, or fear of foreigners, in a category titled ethnicity/national origin. "Ethnicity" refers to a person's membership in a group from a particular country or region of the world who share a common language, customs, and beliefs. For example, Hispanics speak Spanish, are mostly Roman Catholic, and have some similar cultural traditions. "National origin" refers to someone's native country. Hate crimes against immigrants, or people who have a different national origin than native-born Americans, are motivated by the fear that they will weaken or alter their new homeland economically, politically, or culturally.

In 2015, the FBI reported that among racially and ethnically motivated hate crimes, 3.3 percent targeted Latinx. Many other victims were Arab or people who appeared to be Arab. They were targeted because the terrorists who attacked the United States on September 11, 2001, were Arab, an ethnic group from Middle Eastern countries such as Saudi Arabia, Syria, and Iraq. The terrorists were also Muslims, which sparked many religious hate crimes. Not all Arabs, however, are Muslim, and not all Middle Easterners are Arab.

Despite the FBI's statistics, it is believed that many more hate crimes were committed against Latinx, but these crimes were not officially reported. Many Latinx do not report such offenses because they or members of their family are undocumented immigrants, and they fear they could be deported. It is this controversy over the legal status of immigrants, particularly Latinx, that has ignited most of these hate crimes.

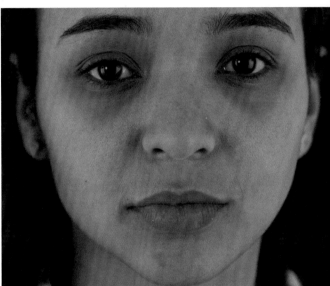

Some Latinx are targeted for hate crimes because of where they come from or the language they speak.

Entering the United States

In August 2006, the Office of Immigration Statistics estimated that more than half of the 11 million people living illegally in the United States—about 6 million—were from Mexico. This realization raised concerns about illegal immigration, such as the ease with which Mexicans could enter the United States and the social cost of caring for them. As of 2014, that number has remained about the same. Anger over this emotional issue combined with ethnic hatred to ignite a wave of violence against Mexicans and other Latinx.

"MERELY BECAUSE OF THE COLOR OF THEIR SKIN"

"The acts alleged in this indictment are senseless.
Individuals were assaulted merely because of the
color of their skin and ethnic background."
—Tim Fuhrman, FBI special agent, on hate-crime
charges filed against three men who attacked a Latino

Quoted in Geoffrey Fattah and Ben Winslow, "Hate-Crimes Crackdown," *Salt Lake City Deseret Morning News*, June 10, 2006, p. B1.

At a public park in Tucson, Arizona, on May 6, 2006, people were celebrating Cinco de Mayo, which commemorates the victory of Mexican forces over occupying French troops in 1862. The peaceful gathering was interrupted by members of the Border Guardians, an anti-immigration group led by Roy Warden. With a pistol strapped to his leg, Warden told the gathered Latinx, "Listen up, Mexican invaders. We will not permit you, the ignorant, the savage, the unwashed, to overrun us. [If] any invader tries to take this land from us we will wash this land and nurture our soil with oceans of their blood!"[54] Warden later sent a threatening email to Isabel Garcia, a Tucson public defender who headed Derechos Humanos, a Latino human-rights group. The email was titled, "Warden to Isabel Garcia: I will blow your ... head off!"[55]

That was one of many Internet threats against Latinx. In June 2006, a group called Save Our States posted a press release on its website "inviting people to go to a day-laborer hiring site in Redondo Beach and to bring their baseball bats."[56] Because many Latinx work as day laborers, it was considered an invitation to beat them. Also available on the Internet were hateful video games that could be downloaded and played. In one game, titled *Border Patrol*, players shot at Mexicans trying to cross the border into the United States.

Ethnic hatred also flares into physical violence. In April 2006, two teenagers in Houston, Texas, were charged with aggravated sexual assault for attacking a 17-year-old Latino boy. In describing the brutal attack, Harris County prosecutor

Mike Trent said, "It looks like they were really trying to kill him and torture him anyway they could."[57] The teens burned their victim's neck with cigarettes, kicked his head, and slashed his chest with a knife because they thought he had kissed a white girl. The girl he kissed was actually Hispanic. The boy did not deserve to be attacked no matter who he kissed, but this shows that hate-crime perpetrators often do not care about the facts of a situation and will use any excuse to attack someone they hate.

Scared to Report

It is believed that many more hate crimes are committed against people with disabilities than are reported. Veronica Robertson, an activist for the disabled community in Chicago, claimed that one reason why many people with disabilities do not report such offenses is because they are afraid of their attackers. "They're scared that the perpetrator will go after them again," Robertson said. In Kathi Wolfe's article "Bashing the Disabled," Robertson recounted how this fear ruined the life of one disabled person:

He's a quadriplegic in his mid-thirties who lives in subsidized housing on the north side of Chicago. Every time he goes outside, the same guy beats him up. While he's beating him, he says, "I don't want you out here, you cripple. I don't like your kind. You people bring down the community." This man is terrified of leaving his apartment building because he knows he'll be beaten and verbally abused. And he's too frightened to report the hate crime because the perpetrator has told him, "If you tell anyone about this, I'll beat your [profanity deleted]."[1]

1. Quoted in Kathi Wolfe, "Bashing the Disabled: The New Hate Crime," *Progressive*, November 1995, p. 8.

Those Who Wear Turbans

Mistaken identity has played a part in many hate crimes following the September 11, 2001, terrorist attacks. In seeking revenge on Muslim Arab terrorists, some perpetrators accidentally targeted non-Muslim Arab Americans as well as people from several countries who were neither Arab nor Muslim. On September 23, 2001, an arson fire at St. George's Assyrian Church in Chicago caused $250,000 in damage. Although the church's members are from Arab countries, they are Christians. Father Charles Klutz said, "The attack against our church is an attack against everyone, regardless of your ethnic background or your religion."[58]

Some Sikhs are targeted by those who believe that anyone who wears a turban is a terrorist.

Five years later, Christian Arabs still feared attacks from people who mistakenly believed they were Muslim. Dany Fahmy lives in the state of Washington. Despite being Christian, Fahmy said in August 2006 that he knew he could be targeted for a hate crime because he has Arabic features. "No one could look at me and tell if I'm an Arabic Christian, an Arabic Southern Baptist, or an Arabic Shi'ite,"[59] he said. His family immigrated to the United States from Beirut, Lebanon, so his father, a Southern Baptist minister, could work with Arab Christians.

People who are neither Arab nor Muslim have been attacked by hate-crime predators who thought they were. On September 15, 2001, Frank Roque shot and killed Balbir Singh Sodhi in Mesa, Arizona. Roque wanted to kill an Arab Muslim in revenge for the attacks by al-Qaeda. Sodhi, however, was from India and was a member of the Sikh religion. Roque thought he was an Arab Muslim because he wore a turban and had a long beard, both of which are Sikh cultural traditions. These features made Sodhi look like Roque's stereotyped conception of Arab Muslims, who sometimes wear head coverings called kaffiyehs and often have beards.

MISUNDERSTANDING

"It's sadly not unknown for Sikh individuals to be targeted as victims of hate crimes by people who perceive them as a quote-unquote terrorist or a quote-unquote Muslim extremist. This crime seems to fit that horrible pattern."
—Jay Boyarsky, prosecutor, commenting on the slaying of Iqbal Singh, a Sikh killed by a neighbor

Quoted in John Cot, "Hate Crime Alleged in Stabbing of Sikh," *San Francisco Chronicle*, August 2, 2006, p. B10.

Many other cases of mistaken identity have occurred. In 2003, several Sikh cab drivers in the San Francisco area were shot to death. Baljit Singh explained why his fellow Sikhs were being targeted: "They just see the turban and the beard and they hate us."[60] Even Sikh children have been targeted. *The Atlantic* reported in 2016 that a nonprofit group called the Sikh Coalition "found that two-thirds of Sikh students get bullied at school. Students reported being accused of hiding grenades or bombs under their head coverings … In a group of 180 students surveyed in Fresno, California, a third said they were bullied because their peers thought they look like terrorists."[61]

Hate Crimes Against People with Disabilities

The same hatred that incited the bullying and killing of Sikhs has been responsible for numerous hate crimes against people with mental and physical disabilities. Just as some people hate others of certain races on sight, some people feel an immediate hatred when they see people with disabilities. According to the FBI, which tallies hate crimes committed against people with disabilities, 57 such incidents occurred in 2004. Thirty-four of these hate crimes involved people with mental disabilities, and 23 involved people with physical disabilities; a total of 73 victims were involved. Kathi Wolfe, who is blind, knows that some people hate the sight of the disabled. She encountered this unreasoning hatred once while entering a subway station in Washington, D.C. Wolfe recalled,

"Move, blind lady," a man hissed at me as he twisted my arm and grabbed my cane. He threw my cane down the escalator. He spat on me and growled, "You people belong in concentration camps." I knew that some people dislike those of us with disabilities, but before this encounter at the subway, I had no idea that this hostility could take the form of such rabid hatred.[62]

People with disabilities are often targeted for hate crimes and bullying.

Mark Sherry also has firsthand knowledge of the prejudices faced by the disabled. His life changed drastically in 1992 after he was run over by a car in his native Australia. In addition to serious internal injuries, Sherry suffered a brain injury that left him disabled by recurring epileptic seizures. As a result, Sherry dedicated his life to researching issues affecting people with disabilities, such as hate crimes. One disturbing fact that Sherry has learned is how much some people hate the disabled. He said this hatred is evident in many ways, from angry stares directed at disabled people in public places to websites that express revulsion for them. Sherry, who has taught at several U.S. universities, wants the world to understand this hatred: "I want people to recognize that hate exists toward disabled people. Often people's assumption is that people have condescension or pity [for the disabled]. But nondisabled people do not want to acknowledge that they hate disabled people, that they hate our difference."[63]

REGARDLESS OF THEIR DISABILITY

"Regardless of [their] cognitive disability people do not deserve to have signs pointed at them, making fun of them, scaring them, harassing them."
—Fraser Nelson, executive director of the Disability Law Center

Quoted in Sam Penrod, "Derogatory Sign Offends Family in Nephi," *Salt Lake City Deseret News*, July 2006, p. B4.

All Walks of Life, a rights group for disabled people in Houston, Texas, also works to educate the public about issues affecting people with disabilities. The group explains that physical problems make some disabled people easy prey for hate-crime perpetrators:

The main cause of violence to people with disabilities is vulnerability. Vulnerability to predators who take advantage of people with developmental, mental and physical disabilities. They are not as able at defending, resisting and/or reporting a physical attack as their nondisabled peers because of their disability.[64]

An example of how this vulnerability works against the disabled occurred in Milltown, New Jersey. On January 30, 1999, Eric Krochmaluk, who is cognitively disabled, accepted an invitation from acquaintances who told him, "Come to a party, you might meet a nice girl."[65] At the party, eight men and women kept Krochmaluk prisoner while they shaved his eyebrows, beat him, burned him with a cigarette, and choked him. Krochmaluk went to the party even though the same people had abused him in the past; because of his disability, he was unable to comprehend that they might hurt him again.

Another incident happened to Jean Parker, a past executive director of the Colorado Cross-Disability Coalition, who is blind. She recalled, "Someone silently approached and deliberately kicked my guide dog in the kidneys."[66] Parker could not see the attacker, which meant she had no way to stop the assault or identify the perpetrator.

Parker's lack of sight also meant that she had no way to identify the hate-crime perpetrator. Mark Sherry believes the trouble that disabled people have in reporting hate crimes is one reason why thousands of such offenses are never reported. "If you believe [FBI statistics], disabled people have less than one in a million chance of experiencing a hate crime. I think that's pure fantasy,"[67] he said. Sherry's claim is based on the fact that even though there are more than 53 million disabled people in the United States, only a handful of crimes against them are reported each year. He believes that as many as 10,000 hate crimes are actually committed annually against the disabled.

What About the Homeless?

Although at least some hate crimes against the disabled are reported, acts of violence against another group—the homeless—are not even considered hate crimes by the federal government or most states. Many people, however, believe they should be because the homeless are regularly targeted for offenses that are generally considered hate crimes. The National Coalition for the Homeless (NCH) reported that in 2015, there were 77 attacks against homeless people, including 27 that resulted in death. That was a decrease from 122 attacks in 2014, when 26 people were killed. However, in the first week of July 2016 alone, four men were attacked, two of whom were set on fire.

Attacked in the Streets

In June 2006, the National Coalition for the Homeless issued a report on violence against the homeless that occurred the previous year. This is an excerpt from that report:

In February [2005], Maria Catherine King, a homeless woman of less than 100 pounds who had been struggling with mental illness, was brutally beaten and killed in Berkeley, California. The suspects were two 18-year-old males. [In] May, in Holly Hill, Florida, five teenagers charged with killing a homeless man said they did it "for fun" because they "needed something to do." The five teens left the scene and returned numerous times to beat Michael Roberts, 53, with their fists, tree branches, and a large log.

In August, in Los Angeles, two 19-year-old men [took] to the streets, hitting sleeping homeless people with aluminum baseball bats and leaving an elderly man in critical condition. Sadly, these gruesome accounts are just a few of many that demonstrate the hate/violence faced by people experiencing homelessness each year.[1]

1. "Hate, Violence, and Death on Main Street USA: A Report on Hate Crimes and Violence Against People Experiencing Homelessness, 2005," National Coalition for the Homeless, June 2006. www.nationalhomeless.org/getinvolved/projects/hatecrimes/index.html.

Several homeless people die each year this way. On March 5, 2006, one homeless man escaped such a death in Boston after he was doused with lighter fluid and set ablaze in a city park. "I was screaming. I could feel my skin melting. I just kicked off my shoes and shucked my pants off. Oh, it hurt,"[68] said the man, who suffered second-degree burns on his left leg. Michael Stoops of the NCH said that arson and baseball-bat beatings "are the two most common forms" of violence against the homeless. Stoops contended, "If this were happening to anyone else, there'd be an uproar. It really baffles me."[69]

Crimes against the homeless are similar to those against the disabled in an important way: Members of both groups are easy to attack. Karen LaFrazia is executive director of St. Francis House, a homeless shelter in Boston. "Homeless people by virtue of their living situation are very vulnerable. They are easy targets for angry people,"[70] she said. According to LaFrazia, every week a few of the people she cares for, most of them women, report they have been attacked.

Multiple homeless people die every year after being intentionally set on fire. Although this is not legally considered a hate crime, hate is the motivating factor.

To prevent such attacks, it is important to gain an understanding of the people who commit hate crimes. For some individuals, differences in race, religion, ethnicity, ability, and sexual orientation can bring about feelings of fear and hatred, which often erupt in violence. For others, prejudices have been instilled since childhood and are difficult to overcome. Recognizing the characteristics common to all hate-crime perpetrators is an important step in combating hate crimes.

The Haters

Arno Michaelis was once an angry teenager who listened to white power music. At 17, he became involved in the white supremacist movement and helped found the Hammerskins, which became the largest racist skinhead organization in the world. He roamed the streets with his friends, beating up people of color or white anti-racists whom he accused of being "race traitors." Today, he has left racism behind, has founded organizations dedicating to building empathy, and works to help others escape from hate groups. Michaelis wrote,

> By the time I turned 16, I was an alcoholic and very comfortable with hate and violence. I hated the town I lived in. I hated my school and most of the teachers and other kids. I hated the police. I discovered racist skinhead music through the punk scene and learned that the swastika is an effective way of angering others—the hostility I radiated was reflected by the people around me, validating the paranoid ideology that had become my identity.[71]

Arno Michaelis is an example of someone who was able to overcome hate and begin to build bridges instead. Like many perpetrators of hate-filled violence, Michaelis was a young man who had a lot of anger and loneliness. He connected with others who gave him someone to blame for how he was feeling. After the birth of his daughter and after one of his skinhead friends was killed as a result of gang activity, he realized he would either end up in prison or dead if he continued down his current path. Not wanting to leave his daughter without a father, he began the process of leaving the racist gang. Now, he speaks and writes about how people can be drawn into hate groups and what it takes to leave them.

Not all perpetrators of hate crimes are members of hate groups like Arno Michaelis. Some act alone. More often now,

Arno Michaelis (left) used to be a white supremacist, but now he speaks out against hate groups.

they participate in online communities where they discuss violence and hate anonymously with strangers on the Internet. Many perpetrators of hate crimes are young; in fact, according to the FBI *Hate Crime Statistics*, 15.3 percent of offenders in 2015 were under 18 years old. In order to prevent hate crimes, it is important to understand what drives those who commit them.

Fighting a Misguided War

The two most common factors that hate-crime perpetrators share are youth and a link to a hate group. Due to their success in appealing to young people, hate groups experienced a surge in membership during the early 21st century. The SPLC tracks the activities of hate groups through its Intelligence Project, which publishes the *Intelligence Report*. The center reported that in 2016, there were 917 active U.S. hate groups. The groups all spread hate speech; many of them advocate violence against blacks, Jews, Muslims, Latinx, and LGBT+; and a few commit hate crimes.

Most hate groups fit into three main categories: neo-Nazis, such as the National Socialist Movement (NSM); the KKK and other racist groups; and skinheads, whose members are mainly young people. These groups all believe in white supremacy. Typical of their racial beliefs are those of the Creativity Movement, which was once known as the World Church of the Creator. The Creativity Movement's motto is "RaHoWa," short for "Racial Holy War." Its members claim that people who are not white are "sub-human" and "natural" enemies of white people, and the group's goal is "survival, expansion, and advancement of [the] White Race exclusively."[72]

The Alt-Right

The alternative right—frequently called the alt-right for short—is "a new term for an informal and ill-defined collection of internet-based radicals."[1] Many people who consider themselves part of the alt-right use the Internet to post things that are racist, sexist, or anti-immigrant. Not all members of the alt-right believe the same thing, but most believe in preserving their idea of white identity. For this reason, most oppose letting non-white people immigrate to the United States. The *New York Times* attempted to define their views:

There is no obvious catchall word for them. The word "racist" has been stretched to cover an attitude toward biology, a disposition to hate, and a varying set of policy preferences, from [racial profiling in] policing to repatriating [deporting] illegal immigrants. While everyone in this set of groups is racist in at least one of these senses, many are not racist in others. Not many ... favored the term "white supremacist." The word implies a claim to superiority—something few insisted on. "White nationalist" is closer to the mark; most people in this part of the alt-right think whites either ought to have a nation or constitute one already. But they feel that almost all words tend to misdescribe or stigmatize them.[2]

1. Christopher Caldwell, "What the Alt-Right Really Means," *New York Times*, December 2, 2016. www.nytimes.com/2016/12/02/opinion/sunday/what-the-alt-right-really-means.html.
2. Caldwell, "What the Alt-Right Really Means."

The KKK and the NSM are two of the biggest hate groups and have been active for many years. In 2016, the KKK had an estimated 130 groups with names such as the Imperial Klans of America and the Mystic Knights; the NSM is the largest neo-Nazi group in the country, with 61 chapters as of 2009. There are no solid membership figures for these groups, but it is believed that they have thousands of members in the United States. In the early 21st century, organizations such as the Border Guardians and Texas Minutemen were created to oppose illegal immigration. Although illegal immigration is a legitimate issue, some people have joined these groups because they hate all Mexicans, even those who are U.S. citizens.

Members of the KKK sometimes dress in these outfits to hide their identity.

There are also many small hate groups. One is the Westboro Baptist Church (WBC) in Topeka, Kansas, whose members hate homosexuals because they believe the Bible condemns them. In protests at the funerals of soldiers killed in the Iraq War, members carried signs that read, "Thank God for Dead Soldiers." They claimed the deaths were a punishment from God because the United States tolerates homosexuality. The protests were universally condemned because they added to the suffering of the families and friends who were already mourning the deaths of loved ones.

FINDING SUPPORTERS

"Not everybody who is receptive contacts us. Some people will just start visiting our website and listening to our radio broadcasts. Some will become active supporters of our cause; others will become passive supporters."
—A leader of the white supremacist organization Arizona National Vanguard, commenting on what people do after they receive a flyer from the group

Quoted in Chip Berlet, "The Hard Edge of Hatred," *Nation*, August 15, 2006. www.thenation.com/doc/20060828/new_nativism.

Recruitment

Whereas the WBC has only a few members, hate groups such as the KKK and the NSM have much larger memberships, in part because they have sophisticated ways to attract followers. One strategy is to stage controversial events to get media coverage. On October 16, 2005, the NSM held a rally in a black section of Toledo, Ohio, because it hoped its presence would incite a violent counterprotest. When blacks and other people who opposed the group's racist creed attacked NSM members, police had to arrest 60 people to protect the neo-Nazis. Millions of people read stories or viewed television coverage of the event, which helped make people aware of the group. NSM leader Jeff Schoep also claimed the violence proved his group's racist theory that black people are savage.

The Stormfront White Nationalist Community pioneered one of the most powerful tactics to win converts. In March 1995, the group started the first hate website. The website was created by Don Black, a former Klansman who believed the new technology would allow hate groups to easily communicate with many more people. Today, Stormfront is no longer alone in spreading hatred. In 2005, the *Intelligence Report* counted 524 hate websites—a 12 percent increase from 468 a year earlier. As of 2017, there are too many to keep track of. Mark Potok, the magazine's editor, once explained that the "veritable explosion of hate sites" since Stormfront began is due to the ease with which the Internet allows them to promote their ideas:

> A few years ago, a Klansman needed to put out substantial effort and money to produce and distribute a shoddy pamphlet that might reach a few hundred people. Today, with a $500 computer and negligible other costs, that same Klansman can put up a slickly produced Web site with a potential audience in the millions.[73]

Teenagers and young adults often visit hate websites out of idle curiosity about such groups or because of a fascination with the symbols they use, such as the Nazi swastika. Hate

Many people are recruited to hate groups through the Internet.

groups welcome young people, who are often too naive to understand that the racist and hateful messages their websites present are based on lies and faulty stereotypes.

Hate groups also try to recruit young people with "white power" music. Panzerfaust Records in South St. Paul, Minnesota, is one of several companies that produce hard-rock music with white-supremacy messages. Groups that sing the songs also perform at rallies. Prussian Blue was a duo of fraternal twins Lynx and Lamb Gaede. In 2005, the 14-year-old blonde, blue-eyed sisters appeared at rallies for Kulturkampf, a neo-Nazi anti-immigrant group. They once claimed in an interview that the most pressing problem today is "not having enough white babies born to replace ourselves and generally not having good-quality white people being born."[74] Their songs have titles such as "Aryan Man Awake," a song that encourages white (Aryan) men to commit violence against people of color.

Jonathan Bernstein of the Anti-Defamation League said such tactics have helped lure young people to hate groups. He said many young people become skinheads after being exposed to such racist commentary. According to Bernstein, "Skinheads are often the foot soldiers for the leaders of the hate movement. They are responsible for much of the hate violence."[75]

"HATE CRIMES ARE DIFFERENT"

"Hate crimes are different from other crimes. They strike at the heart of one's identity … They strike at our sense of self, our sense of belonging. The end result is loss: loss of trust, loss of dignity and, in the worst case, loss of life."

—James Comey, former FBI director

Quoted in Doug Criss, "When Is a Crime a Hate Crime and When Is It Terrorism?," CNN, April 19, 2017. www.cnn.com/2017/04/19/us/hate-crime-or-terrorism-definition-trnd/

Skinheads

Skinheads are the most well-known group of young hate-crime perpetrators. Members of such groups have many things in common, as the FBI has learned. The FBI conducted a seven-year study of racist skinhead groups such as California's Nazi Low Riders. The study showed that most members are uneducated white males between 13 and 24 years of age who are unemployed or have low-paying jobs, and their main form of recreation is getting drunk and taking drugs. When they are high, skinheads often go looking for people to beat up. Because they have learned from their families, friends, or society to hate people who are different, their victims are generally members of the black, Latinx, Jewish, or gay communities. Hate-crime expert Jack Levin explained the psychological rage that fuels such violence: "They're not doing well in school, they see little hope for their future, but in hate they feel special, they feel important at [their victim's] expense. They're bored, they're idle and they're looking to feel a little excitement and this is how they choose to do it."[76]

Skinheads are generally from poor families in big cities. However, Levin notes that, starting in the 1990s, an increasing number of youthful hate-crime perpetrators have come from middle-class and wealthy suburban areas. Levin believes this increase coincides with an increase of minority families moving into the suburbs. He claimed, "These [suburban] kids aren't prepared for people who are different. They see them as a threat. They come home in the afternoon to their empty houses, log onto the Internet, visit hate sites, chat rooms, bulletin boards and get ideas."[77]

Skinhead Gangs

Between 1992 and 1999, the FBI conducted an investigation of skinhead gangs in California to learn more about the violent youths who often commit hate crimes. FBI agents interviewed hundreds of skinheads for the study. One of the skinheads they interviewed belonged to the Nazi Low Riders in Lancaster, California. Gang members prowled the streets of Lancaster in search of minorities, whom they would beat and sometimes stab; they were also linked to the murder of an African American. The following comments, excerpted from the March 2003 *FBI Law Enforcement Bulletin*, are from a 15-year-old who was considered a typical gang member:

I dropped out of school in the eighth grade, but I stopped learning midway through the sixth grade. I covered my body with hate tattoos. I couldn't get a good job if I wanted to. No one would hire me. Once, I tried to get a job at a fast food restaurant, but the manager refused to hire me because the restaurant served multiracial customers. If I quit being a skinhead, I have nothing. I am nothing. I have no choice but to be a skinhead. I expect to die a young, violent death.[1]

1. Quoted in Joe Navarro and John R. Schafer, "The Seven-Stage Hate Model: The Psychopathy of Hate Groups," *FBI Law Enforcement Bulletin*, March 2003, p. 5.

An example of hate crimes committed by such young people occurred in Alabama in February 2006, when three Birmingham-Southern College students were arrested in a string of arson fires at churches, several of them with black congregations. Initially, officials believed the fires were set by the KKK or other hate groups. "This is just so hard to believe. My profile on these suspects is shot all to heck and back,"[78] state fire marshal Richard W. Montgomery said when he learned the students were responsible for the fires. Montgomery was shocked because the students—one of them the son of a doctor—were so unlike most of the people who have committed such crimes in the past.

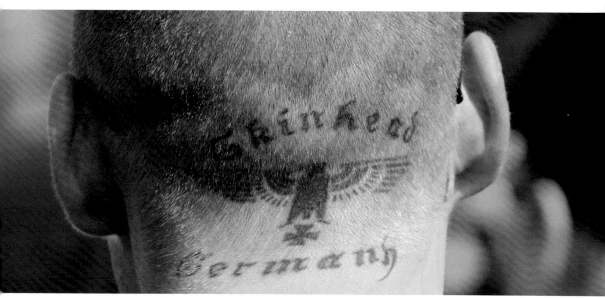

Skinheads sometimes display their membership in the gang through tattoos, such as the one pictured here.

Police Violence

Although teens and young adults are responsible for nearly half of all hate crimes, many older adults also commit them. Sometimes the people expected to uphold the law are the ones committing the crimes. There have been a few high-profile cases of police officers committing hate crimes, and some studies suggest that this is a problem that often goes unreported. One group often targeted by law enforcement officials is the LGBT+ community. In 2005, Amnesty International (AI), which tracks human-rights violations worldwide, issued a 159-page report on such hate crimes. AI spokesman William F. Schulz said, "Across the country [such people] endure the injustices of discrimination, entrapment and verbal abuse, as well as brutal beatings and sexual assault at the hands of those responsible for protecting them—the police."[79] One incident cited in the AI report involved the way New York officers treated a transgender man whom they had arrested. According to the report, after placing him in a cell for women, "officers walked past him repeatedly, mocking his name and asking, 'What is this thing?'"[80]

Other incidents that raise concern are those in which white police officers use excessive force when arresting African Americans. One infamous case involved Rodney King, who, on March 3, 1991, was brutally attacked by Los Angeles, California, police officers when they arrested him for speeding. The officers claimed that King was resisting arrest and that they were only doing what was necessary to subdue him. The incident, however, had been videotaped by a bystander. When it was shown on television, it created a firestorm of controversy about police brutality. In 1992, when the four officers charged with using excessive force to subdue King were found not guilty, black people in Los Angeles were so angry that they erupted in one of the city's worst riots.

The King beating was one of many videotaped incidents involving white officers who appeared to use excessive force when arresting African Americans. Many of those incidents have resulted in the death of the victims. One incident happened in July 2014, when Eric Garner, a black man, was killed by police as they arrested him. Garner was put in a chokehold, even though he was not behaving violently and, despite telling the officers several times that he could not breathe, was not given medical attention afterward. An autopsy—a medical examination conducted to determine the cause of a person's death—showed that the chokehold and pressure to the chest were responsible for Garner's death. The arresting officers defended their actions, but after viewing video of the incident that had been taken with an onlooker's cell phone, many people believed the police had used excessive force and ignored Garner's pleas for help.

Police are more likely to hurt or shoot an unarmed black person than a white one because of fears that the black person is more likely to become violent. Many unarmed black people, especially black men, have been shot when police mistakenly believed the victim was reaching for a gun. These fears are based on racist beliefs that police officers may not even be entirely aware of, but they influence behavior nonetheless. Some people say race is not an issue in these cases because police also shoot unarmed white people. However, as the *Chicago Tribune* reported in July 2016,

According to the most recent census data, there are nearly 160 million more white people in America than there are black people. White people make up roughly 62 percent of the U.S. population but only about 49 percent of those who are killed by police officers. African Americans, however, account for 24 percent of those fatally shot and killed by the police despite being just 13 percent of the U.S. population. As The Post noted in a new analysis published last week, that means black Americans are 2.5 times as likely as white Americans to be shot and killed by police officers …

And, when considering shootings confined within a single race, a black person shot and killed by police is more likely to have been unarmed than a white person. About 13 percent of all black people who have been fatally shot by police since January 2015 were unarmed, compared with 7 percent of all white people.[81]

Native Americans are even more likely to face violence from police than black people, although this issue often goes unreported by the media. In many of these instances, the police are not charged with a crime. People of all races have recently begun campaigning for police reform and accountability; they want police who use excessive force to be charged with assault or murder.

Black Lives Matter is a group that protests against police brutality and draws attention to the role of the police in hate crimes.

IT STARTS WITH YOU

"You cannot hate other people without
hating yourself."
—Oprah Winfrey, TV personality

Quoted in "10 Quotes That Encourage Us to Stand Up Against Hate Crime," Crimestoppers,
June 29, 2016. blog.crimestoppers-uk.org/10-quotes-encourage-us-stand-hate-crime/.

Although some police officers are unaware of their racist beliefs, others belong to racist groups. The Nebraska State Patrol
fired Robert Henderson on June 26, 2006, because he was a
member of the KKK. Nebraska attorney general Jon Bruning said
at the time, "We don't want the agency destroyed by a racist like
Bob Henderson."[82] On August 18, 2006, however, a state labor
arbitrator reinstated Henderson after ruling that the dismissal
violated the trooper's constitutional right to free speech.

The Role of Community Leaders in Preventing Hate

When a hate crime occurs, one of the most powerful things government and community leaders can do is condemn the offense.
Hate-crime experts Jack Levin and Jack McDevitt explained why:

*First of all, community leaders must speak out condemning the
attack. This is important because it sends two essential messages: to
the victims, that local residents want them to remain members of that
community and, to the offenders, that most people in the community do not support their illegal behavior. Interviews with hate crime
offenders indicate that they frequently believe that most of the community shares their desire to eliminate the "outsider." The offenders
often see themselves as heroes or at least as "cool" in the eyes of their
friends, because they have the courage to act on what they believe
to be commonly held beliefs. Public statements by local community
leaders challenge this idea and send a message to offenders that
their actions are not supported.[1]*

1. Jack Levin and Jack McDevitt, "Hate Crimes," Brudnick Center on Violence and Conflict, Northeastern University.
www.violence.neu.edu/publication4.html.

The Cowardice of Hate Crimes

There are many types of people who commit hate crimes, but some people claim these perpetrators all have one thing in common: They are cowards. On July 29, 2006, three men used baseball bats and knives to assault five gay men in San Diego, California. Two days later, when San Diego mayor Jerry Sanders promised to find the men, he said, "I have a few choice words for the criminals who committed this vicious attack—you are cowards."[83] Even though the gay men outnumbered their attackers, Sanders labeled the attackers cowards because their victims were unarmed. Studies have shown, however, that perpetrators generally outnumber victims in hate crimes. That is why many people accuse them of cowardice; people believe they would not pick a fight if the victims were better able to defend themselves.

An example of this was evident in Utah on November 3, 2005, when U.S. attorney Paul Warner charged three whites with beating a black man. In announcing the charges, Warner questioned their bravery: "These people are cowards. They attack at night, they attack in the dark, they attack in overwhelming numbers."[84]

Hate crimes often involve large, armed groups against defenseless individuals, causing some to say that hate crime perpetrators are cowards.

What Can People Do to Stop the Hate?

Given the harm that hate crimes cause to everyone involved—the victims, the perpetrators, and the entire community—it is vital that people take steps to try to end them. Everyone has a role to play in preventing hate crimes.

Society's laws define what is and is not acceptable behavior. Hate crimes are against the law because of the great harm that they do to the country as a whole. Laws that impose strict penalties for hate crimes are one way of preventing the crimes from occurring. Citizens should encourage lawmakers to keep hate-crime legislation up to date and make it a priority.

Organizations also play a role in preventing hate crimes. The SPLC tracks hate crimes and hate groups all around the country. There are other organizations working to end hate crimes and build empathy as well. Anti-bullying programs in schools may help stop future hate-crime perpetrators before they ever start.

Individuals can also do a lot to fight hate crimes. By speaking out against hatred, reaching out to people who are different, and educating themselves and others about the problem, people can be allies in the fight against prejudice. Some individual survivors of hate crimes or the families of victims have founded organizations that are doing great work to begin to eliminate these horrible crimes so others will not have to suffer as they have. If someone witnesses or experiences a hate crime, they can do their part by reporting it to the police or to organizations that track instances of hate crimes all around the country. By working together, everyone can reduce the violence in their communities.

Hate Crimes and the Law

Although federal and state governments can outlaw hate crimes, they can never end the hatred that causes them. Such laws, however, can sufficiently punish perpetrators to make people think twice before committing such offenses. In 2017, every state except Wyoming had laws against hate crimes, although not all of these laws cover all types of hate crimes. For instance, 20 states do not have laws that cover hate crimes against LGBT+ people. Some states have created new criminal offenses for hate crimes, and others have simply increased penalties for existing crimes in which the offenses can also be considered hate crimes. Both types of laws result in longer jail or prison sentences.

There is also a federal law called the Matthew Shepard and James Byrd Jr. Hate Crimes Prevention Act, which President Obama signed into law in 2009. In 2017, Joshua Vallum of Mississippi became the first person to be prosecuted under the federal law for a crime against a transgender person. Vallum killed his ex-girlfriend Mercedes Williamson in 2015 because she was a transgender woman and he was worried his own life would be in danger if the other members of his gang, the Latin Kings, found out he had dated her. Vallum was charged by the state of Mississippi with murder, but since Mississippi's hate-crime laws do not cover crimes against LGBT+ people, he was also prosecuted under the federal Hate Crimes Act.

Some officials believe harsher punishment is necessary because hate crimes affect society as a whole. On July 17, 2006, Nicholas Minucci was sentenced to 15 years in prison for beating Glenn Moore, a black man walking through his Howard Beach, New York, neighborhood. He also stole Moore's shoes. Minucci's sentence was nearly twice the state-allowed minimum for the charges of robbery and assault if the offense had not been a hate crime. Queens, New York, district attorney Richard Brown explained why the longer prison term was justified: "The sentence reflect[s] an understanding of the fact that when Nicholas Minucci picked up that aluminum baseball bat on June 29 of last year in Howard Beach, he raised that bat against not only Glenn Moore, but against every other resident of this city."[85]

Most state laws add extra punishment for hate crimes motivated by race, religion, or ethnicity. As of 2017, however, some states still did not include sexual orientation as a hate-crime motivation, others did not include gender identity, and few covered homeless people. The lack of protection for the homeless was highlighted in Fort Lauderdale, Florida, on January 12, 2006, when three teenagers were charged with first-degree murder after they used a baseball bat to kill Norris Gaynor, who was homeless. The attack, which was recorded by a surveillance camera, gained worldwide attention when it was shown on television newscasts. Gaynor's brutal slaying made many people believe such offenses should be considered hate crimes.

It is important that individual states include gender identity, sexual orientation, and homelessness under their hate crimes legislation because the federal role in prosecuting hate crimes is limited. The U.S. government does not prosecute many hate crimes because it believes that is the role of states. However, the federal government fights hate crimes by compiling hate-crime statistics, educating the public on hate crimes, and assisting hate-crime victims through agencies such as the U. S. Department of Justice's Community Relations Service.

Local governments also fight hate crimes. Officials in Fairfax, Virginia, print and distribute a brochure in six languages so hate-crime victims who do not speak English will know how to report offenses. Likewise, on May 17, 2006, Boulder, Colorado, became the first city in the nation to authorize a hate-crime hotline. That telephone service was similar to many that private groups were already operating in many cities.

Laws play an important role in preventing hate crimes. People who are charged with hate crimes may receive harsher punishments.

How Young Adults Can Fight Hate

The National Youth Violence Prevention Resource Center website has information on hate crimes. Here are some suggestions on how young people can try to stop hate crimes:

Start with yourself. Try to broaden your social circle to include others who are different from you. Be mindful of your language—avoid stereotypical remarks and challenge those made by others. Speak out against jokes and slurs that target people or groups. Silence sends a message that you are in agreement. It is not enough to refuse to laugh.

Read books about diverse cultures, traditions, and lifestyles in our society ...

Talk with your friends, parents, and school staff about how you and your classmates can respond to hateful attitudes and behaviors ... Research and find out about hate crimes that have occurred in your community and what was done to respond to them. Identify any hate groups active in your community ...

Join an existing group that is promoting tolerance in your school or community, or launch your own effort. Join with other students to create anti-hate policies and programs in your school.[1]

1. "What You Can Do," National Youth Violence Prevention Resource Center. www.safeyouth.org/scripts/teens/hate.asp.

The Legal Fight Against Hate

In addition to telephone hotlines, private organizations use a variety of methods and approaches to combat hate crimes. The SPLC has battled hate crimes since it was founded in 1971 to help black people gain their civil rights. It monitors hate-crime activity; publicizes offenses in its quarterly magazine, the *Intelligence Report*; and uses legal action to cripple hate groups such as the KKK. In 1988, the SPLC won nearly $1 million in damages for 11 Georgia residents who had been attacked by members of the

Invisible Empire Knights. Once one of the nation's largest and most violent KKK groups, the court decision left the Invisible Empire bankrupt and forced it to disband.

SPREADING TOLERANCE

"That is not what California stands for. The greatness of California is its rich diversity. Hate, racism and intolerance are never accepted in our public debates. I encourage all people to spread the good word of tolerance."
—Arnold Schwarzenegger, former governor of California, commenting on hate threats against Mexican American public officials

Arnold Swarzenegger, "Governor Arnold Schwarzenegger's Remarks at Executive Order Signing for Crime Victim Advocate," Office of the Governor, April 24, 2006. www.gov.ca.gov/index.php/speech/160.

Another powerful hate-crime opponent is the Anti-Defamation League (ADL), which was founded in 1913. It has one of the most comprehensive and informative hate-crime websites, and it monitors hate crimes through its many local offices. The ADL is one of many organizations that directly represent groups of people who are targeted for hate crimes. Other organizations include the American-Arab Anti-Discrimination Committee, the National Association for the Advancement of Colored People (NAACP), the Asian American Legal Defense and Education Fund, and Parents and Friends of Lesbians and Gays. The ADL stresses, however, that everyone, not just possible victims, should be concerned about hate crimes: "All Americans have a stake in an effective response to violent bigotry. Hate crimes demand a priority response because of their special emotional and psychological impact on the victim and the victim's community. [Such] incidents can damage the fabric of our society and fragment communities."[86]

One of those situations that could rip a community apart occurred in Seattle, Washington, on July 28, 2006, when Naveed Afzal Haq, a Muslim, killed 58-year-old Pamela Waechter and wounded several other Jewish people in a shooting rampage at the Jewish Federation of Greater Seattle.

To heal the wound caused by the shooting, people of all faiths attended Waechter's July 31 funeral. "All lives are sacred,"[87] said Joy Carey, a Muslim. Andy Hoskins, an Episcopalian who attended, said, "I want people here [in the Jewish community] to know they have friends everywhere."[88] The show of support helped keep Seattle from being divided by hate.

Groups such as the ADL, the Council on American-Islamic Relations, and Lambda Legal, which mainly works with gay, lesbian, bisexual, and transgender people, also help victims cope with hate crimes. The groups help victims report hate crimes to the authorities, and many operate hate-crime hotlines. The groups also provide medical assistance and counseling for victims and advise them of their legal rights, such as what to do if their attacker is arrested and charged with the crime.

Groups must work together to prevent hate crimes.

Hate Crimes Online

In the 21st century, people are more connected than ever before. Sometimes this leads to wonderful results, such as making new friends around the globe. Other times, however, the Internet can be a platform for people to spread hatred. Social media and personalized websites make it quick and easy for hate groups to connect with new members as well as plan organized demonstrations.

Unfortunately, online harassment is difficult to stop. People can target others anywhere in the world, which means it is not always clear which police force has jurisdiction. Some of these people are skilled at hiding their location, so law enforcement agencies may not even be able to find them.

Many online hate crimes involve threats against women. The *Telegraph* reported that "many women in public life have pointed out the online abuse they receive is not directed at what they have said or done, but at their gender. Sprinkled in amongst the general abuse and bomb threats has been a recurring motif: misogynistic and sexualised language and—almost invariably—threats of rape."[89] The Greater Manchester Police in England received complaints in 2014 about 38 online threats of murder and 8 reports of rape involving girls under the age of 16. Several European countries are taking online hate crimes seriously; the United Kingdom (UK) has set up a special police force to target Internet trolls, and in 2017, Germany approved a bill that would fine online hate speech perpetrators as much as 50 million euros (53.4 million U.S. dollars). Some people hope the United States will take similar steps.

Because it is so difficult to find people who commit hate crimes online, many perpetrators go uncaught and unpunished. However, a few cases have been brought to trial in the past. In the 1990s, a college student named Kingman Quon sent threatening and insulting messages to Hispanic people across the country, including 25 students at the Massachusetts Institute of Technology (MIT). In 1999, the Department of Justice charged Quon with violating the students' civil rights and sentenced him to two years in prison.

In another case, a white supremacist named Ryan Wilson was charged by the Commonwealth of Pennsylvania with posting threatening and harassing messages on his website. In 1998, the court ordered the website taken down and banned Wilson from posting those kinds of messages online.

The Importance of Education

One of the most important things anti-hate groups do is educate people about hate crimes. The ways in which they do this are almost limitless. Groups maintain websites; print publications; and sponsor speeches, lectures, and other public events. These educational efforts are aimed not only at the general public but also at specialized audiences. The SPLC and the ADL both offer classes for law enforcement officials and teachers.

WORKING TOGETHER

"This place is a place of worship. It's a place where people come to seek love and care. As a Muslim, I'm cleaning a Jewish building because my religion tells me: Respect every religion and religious place."
–Saeed Shahzad, discussing why he was cleaning swastikas off Striar Jewish Community Center in Stoughton, Massachusetts

Quoted in Michael Levenson, "In Stoughton, They Join Hands to Wash Out Hate," *Boston Globe*, March 6, 2006, p. B2.

However, Debra Chasnoff, president and senior producer of GroundSpark, believes that students are the most important group that should be educated. Chasnoff, an Oscar-winning filmmaker, has directed several videos through GroundSpark's Respect for All Project that explain hate crimes and show how people can become more tolerant of those who are different. In *Let's Get Real*, students who have been bullied because of race, religion, disabilities, or sexual orientation explain what happened to them and how they felt. The video includes interviews with student bullies who have realized that what they did was wrong. Chasnoff believes young people need to learn such lessons because school bullying is similar in many ways to hate crimes:

> We can no longer sit back and dismiss bullying as a rite of passage that all kids just have to live through. Unchecked bullying compromises student performance, damages physical and mental health, and perpetuates a cycle that can escalate to even greater, more brutal forms of violence, including hate crimes.[90]

Clinton Sipes could have benefited from hate-crime education when he was growing up. He said, "I think if someone had come and told me, tried to teach me some things about people, I might have felt differently. I wouldn't have been so angry, but no one ever did."[91]

The fight against hate crimes can start at school.

An educational program that has helped entire communities fight hate crimes is Not In Our Town (NIOT). In 1993, in Billings, Montana, white supremacists desecrated a Jewish cemetery, painted swastikas on a Native American family's house, and broke a window in the home of a family displaying a menorah, which is a Jewish religious symbol. The hate spree lasted several weeks and spurred city officials and community groups to fight back in a collective effort that eventually became NIOT. A labor union painted over the swastikas, and civic organizations staged marches and protests against racism. When the *Billings Gazette* printed pictures of paper menorahs, 10,000 people of all faiths displayed them in their windows.

In 1995, the Public Broadcasting Service (PBS) televised a documentary about Billings titled *Not In Our Town*. Since then, the documentary has inspired people in hundreds of other communities to band together to fight hate crimes. In Contra Costa County, California, Barbara and Ed Tonningsen formed a NIOT group after they saw the film. When a mosque was vandalized after September 11, 2001, group members called Muslims to show their support. NIOT member Susan Hedgpeth said, "That human-to-human connection, that's very powerful, and I think that's how we change things."[92]

Even One Person Can Make a Difference

Such one-on-one contact is a powerful weapon in fighting hate crimes. However, there are many other ways people can make a difference in that battle as well. When her husband was shot to death in 1999, Sherialyn Byrdsong said she had a choice to make: "I had to dig deep and ask myself some questions. Would I let this turn me into a hater?"[93] Instead of hating all white people because one had killed her husband, Byrdsong decided to fight the hatred that led to his death. In the years since then, she has given many speeches in an effort to educate people about hate crimes and their devastating effects.

HATE CRIMES HURT EVERYONE

"Teach your children to accept and understand diversity because the consequences of hate hurt the families of the victim. It also hurts the families of the perpetrators. Lives are ended and lives are changed forever."
—Judy Shepard on the fifth anniversary of the slaying of her son Matthew

Judy Shepard, "Five Years Later, Progress Against Gay Hatred Lags," *USA Today*, October 13, 2003, p. A15.

In 1998, Judy Shepard reacted in the same way after her son Matthew was brutally murdered in Wyoming because he was gay. In countless personal appearances and articles for newspapers and magazines, she has tried to get people to fight the hatred that leads to such crimes even though she knows it is a difficult task. Shepard said, "I'm not naive to think that hate isn't alive and well. We're not born knowing how to do that. If we can learn how to hate, then we can unlearn and replace it with love and respect."[94]

Judy Shepard, whose son was brutally murdered for being gay, now speaks out against hate.

Byrdsong and Shepard are famous because of tragedies that touched them, but ordinary people can also fight hate. Parents are the most important individuals in this battle. Morris Dees helped found the SPLC. Dees believes that he grew up free of the racism that was strong in his native Alabama because of what he learned from his mother and father. He recalled, "My parents treated blacks as equal human beings at a time when my playmates' parents treated them as second-class citizens."[95] The example set by his parents allowed Dees to overcome the racist comments and behavior that he heard and saw while growing up.

"The Kindness of Brave People"

Arno Michaelis, the reformed racist skinhead who now fights for tolerance, wrote,

> I've been beat up as often as I've beaten others, and in no case did being on the receiving end of violence make me any less violent. It was actually the kindness of brave people who refused to lower themselves to my level that changed the course of my life, to put me in a position to follow their example and promote the practice of loving-kindness myself. We cannot hate violent extremism out of existence.[96]

Each person should be treated with love, no matter who they are. By reaching out to others, learning about people who are different, and speaking up against intolerance, the world can be made into a place where hate crimes are unthinkable rather than common.

Introduction: Hate Crimes: An Overview

1. Quoted in Associated Press, "Hate Crime Alleged in Central Florida Bar Attack, Police Say," *Orlando Sentinel*, March 3, 2015. www.orlandosentinel.com/news/breaking-news/os-ap-hate-crime-bar-not-for-blacks-20150303-story.html.

2. Federal Bureau of Investigations, *Hate Crime Statistics 2004*. Washington, DC: U.S. Department of Justice, 2005, p. 10.

3. Elie Wiesel, "We Choose Honor," *Parade Magazine*, October 28, 2001, p. 4.

Chapter 1: Why Do People Hate?

4. Sara Bullard, *Teaching Tolerance: Raising Open-Minded, Empathetic Children*. New York, NY: Doubleday, 1996, p. 27.

5. Bullard, *Teaching Tolerance*, p. 27.

6. Jack Levin and Gordana Rabrenovic, *Why We Hate*. Amherst, NY: Prometheus, 2004, p. 63.

7. Quoted in Robert J. Sternberg, ed., *The Psychology of Hate*. Washington, DC: American Psychological Association, 2005, p. 52.

8. Robert M. Baird and Stuart E. Rosenbaum, eds., *Bigotry, Prejudice, and Hatred: Definitions, Causes, and Solutions*. Amherst, NY: Prometheus, 1992, p. 13.

9. Quoted in Bullard, *Teaching Tolerance*, p. 29.

10. Quoted in Public Broadcasting Service, "Not In Our Town." www.pbs.org/niot/about/niot1.html.

11. Quoted in Gregory M. Herek, "The 'Us' and 'Them' of Murder," University of California, Davis. www.psychology.ucdavis.edu/rainbow/html/shepard.html.

12. Quoted in Levin and Rabrenovic, *Why We Hate*, p. 116.

13. Quoted in John Spong, "The Hate Debate," *Texas Monthly*, April 2001, p. 66.

14. Quoted in Anti-Defamation League, "The Consequences of Right-Wing Extremism on the Internet." www.adl.org/internet/extremism_rw/inspiring.asp.

15. Quoted in "Immigration Fervor Fuels Racist Extremism," Southern Poverty Law Center. www.splcenter.org/news/item.jsp?aid= 186.

16. Jack Levin and Jack McDevitt, "Hate Crimes," Brudnick Center on Violence and Conflict, Northeastern University. www.violence.neu.edu/publication4.html.

Chapter 2: Hated for Their Race

17. Quoted in Vanessa Hua, "Hate Crime Trial Nears End," *San Francisco Chronicle*, July 12, 2004, p. B1.

18. Quoted in Dinesh D'Souza, *The End of Racism: Principles for a Multiracial Society*. New York, NY: Free Press, 1995, p. 27.

19. Quoted in John Asbury, "Swastikas, Satanic Symbols Mar Homes," *Riverside (CA) Press-Enterprise*, July 11, 2006, p. B1.

20. Quoted in Mark Babineck, "Dragging Death Haunts Quiet Texas Town," *Los Angeles Times*, June 8, 2003, p. A20.

21. Quoted in Nicole Sweeney, "Hate Case Brings 176-Year Term," *Milwaukee Journal Sentinel*, April 26, 2002, p. B1.

22. Quoted in Natasha Kaye Johnson, "Assault Stirs Bad Memories," *Gallup Independent*, June 12, 2006. www.gallupindependent.com/2006/jun/061206bdmmrs.html.

23. Quoted in Donald Altschiller, ed., *Hate Crimes: A Reference Handbook*. Santa Barbara, CA: ABC-CLIO, 2005, p. 20.

24. Quoted in Lisa Muñoz, "L.I. Man Faces Hate Crime Rap in Mall Attack," *New York Daily News*, June 7, 2006, p. 19.

25. Quoted in State of Wisconsin, "*State v. Mitchell* 169 Wis. 2d 153 (1992)." www.wicourts.gov/about/organization/supreme/docs/ famouscases20.pdf.

26. Quoted in John Spano, "Hate Crime Charged in Gang Killing," *Los Angeles Times*, June 29, 2006, p. B5.

27. Quoted in George Will, "The Right to Be a Cross-Burning Moron," *Albany Times Union*, April 10, 2003, p. A17.

28. Quoted in Hua, "Hate Crime Trial Nears End," p. B1.

29. Quoted in Kate Hawley, "A Message of Tolerance, Peace; Hate Crime Victim's Widow Speaks at Annual Vigil," *Peoria Journal Star*, April 28, 2006, p. B1.

30. Quoted in Larry Welborn, "Hate Crime Brings 10 Years," *Orange County (CA) Register*, June 24, 2006, p. 1.

31. Quoted in Sweeney, "Hate Case Brings 176-Year Term," p. B1.

Chapter 3: Hated for Their Religion

32. Quoted in Sternberg, ed., *The Psychology of Hate*, p. 52.

33. Quoted in Richard Winton, Andrew Blankstein, and Megan Garvey, "Mel Gibson Charged with Misdemeanor," *Los Angeles Times*, August 2, 2006, p. A1.

34. Quoted in Curt Woodward, "Attack on Center Has Unlikely Hero; Seattle Police Call It a Hate Crime," *Houston Chronicle*, July 30, 2006, p. 3.

35. Eric Lichtblau, "Hate Crimes Against American Muslims Most Since Post-9/11 Era," *New York Times*, September 17, 2016. www.nytimes.com/2016/09/18/us/politics/hate-crimes-american-muslims-rise.html.

36. Quoted in United Nations, "UN Seminar Participants Stress Importance of Tolerance, Understanding, Education in Countering Islamophobia," press release, December 7, 2004. www.un.org/News/Press/docs/2004/hr4801.doc.html.

37. Quoted in "Video Shows Bullet-Riddled Qur'an Thrown at Tennessee Mosque," The American Muslim. www.theamericanmuslim.org/tam.php/features/articles/video_shows_bullet_riddled_quran_thrown_at_tennessee_mosque/009756.

38. Quoted in Scott Williams, "Dolan Stirs Crowd at Holy Hill; Archbishop Tries to Heal Outrage After Site's Vandalism," *Milwaukee (WI) Journal Sentinel*, June 11, 2006, p. B1.

39. Quoted in John Ellement, "Everett Church Vandalism Eyed for Possible Scandal Tie," *Boston Globe*, November 2, 2002, p. B1.

40. Quoted in George Joseph, "Idols Vandalized at Minnesota Temple," *India Abroad*, April 21, 2006, p. A1.

41. Quoted in Marshall Allen, "Baptist Church Vandalized," *San Gabriel Valley (CA) Tribune*, March 14, 2006, p. 1.

Chapter 4: Hated for Their Sexual Orientation or Gender Identity

42. Quoted in Gregory M. Herek, Jeanine C. Cogan, and J. Roy Gillis, "Victim Experiences in Hate Crimes Based on Sexual Orientation," *Journal of Social Issues*, 2002, vol. 58, p. 329.

43. Quoted in John M. Glionna, "Two Guilty of Killing Transgender Teen; the Men Bludgeoned and Choked Gwen Araujo After Accusing Her of Deceiving Them About Her Biological Identification," *Los Angeles Times*, September 13, 2005, p. B1.

44. Dani Heffernan, "Study Shows Anti-LGBT Slurs Still Used for Harm," GLAAD, January 24, 2012. www.glaad.org/blog/study-shows-anti-lgbt-slurs-still-used-harm.

45. Quoted in Steven Elbow, "Four Charged with Hate Crimes," *Madison (WI) Capital Times*, January 18, 2006, p. A10.

46. Quoted in Candace Rondeaux, "Vandalism Damages More than Property; for Gay Couple, Fear Hits Home," *Washington Post*, August 6, 2006, p. T3.

47. Quoted in Herek, Cogan, and Gillis, "Victim Experiences in Hate Crimes Based on Sexual Orientation," p. 333.

48. Quoted in Celeste Katz, "Teen Sought in Wild Attack at Gay Bar," *New York Daily News*, February 3, 2006, p. 12.

49. Quoted in Bob Moser, "'Disposable People,'" *Intelligence Report*, Winter 2003. www.splcenter.org/intel/intelreport/article.jsp?aid =149.

50. Quoted in Chris Summer, "The Victims of Prejudice," BBC News Online. www.news.bbc.co.uk/2/hi/americas/3219591.stm.

51. Quoted in Tom Owens, "Every Story Counts: LGBTQ Activists Rally at Capitol," Teaching Tolerance, March 8, 2006. www.tolerance.org/news/article_tol.jsp?id=1367.

52. Diana Wess, "Hate Speech Disturbs," *Fort Collins Coloradoan*, June 21, 2006, p. 3.

53. Quoted in "Hate Crimes Against Gays," 365Gay.com,

August 9, 2006. www.365gay.com/Newscon06/08/080906 hate.html.

Chapter 5: Hated for Being Different

54. Quoted in "Immigration Fervor Fuels Racist Extremism," Southern Poverty Law Center.

55. Quoted in "Immigration Fervor Fuels Racist Extremism," Southern Poverty Law Center.

56. Quoted in Troy Anderson, "Migrant Debate Spurs Hate," *Whittier (CA) Daily News*, June 5, 2006, p. 8.

57. Quoted in "Immigration Fervor Fuels Racist Extremism," Southern Poverty Law Center.

58. Quoted in *Arab American View*, "Arson Hits Arab Church," November 5, 2001, p. 1.

59. Quoted in Erica Hall, "Local Arab-Americans Face Uphill Battle Against Public Perception," *King County (WA) Journal*, August 24, 2006, p. 1.

60. Quoted in Raj Jayadev, "Sikh Cab Drivers Say Racism, Recession Put Them in the Crosshairs," *Pacific News Service*, October 27, 2003. www.news.pacificnews.org/news/view_article.html.

61. Emma Green, "The Trouble with Wearing Turbans in America," *The Atlantic*, January 27, 2015. www.theatlantic.com/politics/archive/2015/01/the-trouble-with-wearing-turbans-in-america/384832.

62. Kathi Wolfe, "Bashing the Disabled: The New Hate Crime," *Progressive*, November 1995, p. 7.

63. Quoted in Laura Hershey, "Researcher Uses Knowledge to Fight Hate: An Interview with Mark Sherry," *Disability World*, June–August 2003. www.disabilityworld.org/06-08_03/gov/sherry.shtml.

64. Quoted in "Increased Vulnerability to Dangers," All Walks of Life. www.awoltexas.org/dangers.html.

65. Quoted in Hershey, "Researcher Uses Knowledge to Fight Hate."

66. Quoted in Wolfe, "Bashing the Disabled," p. 7.

67. Quoted in Hershey, "Researcher Uses Knowledge to Fight Hate."

68. Quoted in Laurel J. Sweet, "Homeless Man Set on Fire," *Boston Herald*, March 6, 2006, p. 7.

69. Quoted in Sweet, "Homeless Man Set on Fire," p. 7.

70. Quoted in Laura Crimaldi, "Taped Beating of Homeless Man Triggers Hate-Crime Debate," *Boston Herald*, March 5, 2006, p. 5.

Chapter 6: The Haters

71. Arno Michaelis, "This Is How You Become a White Supremacist," *Washington Post*, June 25, 2015. www.washingtonpost.com/posteverything/wp/2015/06/25/this-is-how-you-become-a-white-supremacist/?utm_term=.74ad0cd900ee.

72. "Extremism in America: Creativity Movement," Anti-Defamation League. www.adl.org/Learn/ext_us/WCOTC.asp.

73. Mark Potok, "Internet Hate and the Law," *Intelligence Report*, Winter 2000. www.splcenter.org/intel/intelreport/article.jsp?aid=28 8&.

74. Quoted in Chip Berlet, "The Hard Edge of Hatred," *Nation*, August 15, 2006. www.thenation.com/doc/20060828/new_nativism.

75. Quoted in Carolyne Zinko, Stacy Finz, and Julie N. Lynem, "Firebomb Attempt at San Jose Judge's Home; 3 Teenage Suspects Arrested in Alleged Hate Crime," *San Francisco Chronicle*, August 31, 1999, p. A17.

76. Quoted in Ryan Menard, "Teens Seeking a Thrill," *Quincy (ME) Patriot Ledger*, March 6, 2006, p. 1.

77. Quoted in Bob Moser, "Age of Rage: Young Extremists Find New Targets—and New Recruits," *Intelligence Report*, Summer 2004. www.splcenter.org/intel/intelreport/article.jsp?aid=468.

78. Quoted in Rick Lyman, "Three Students Held in Church Fires Set in Alabama," *New York Times*, March 9, 2006, p. A1.

79. Quoted in *Filipino Reporter*, "Filipino Gay Abused by Cops," October 7–13, 2005, p. 1.

80. Quoted in *Filipino Reporter*, "Filipino Gay Abused by Cops," p. 1.

81. Wesley Lowery, "More Whites Killed by Police, but Blacks 2.5 Times More Likely to Be Killed," *Chicago Tribune*, July 11, 2016. www.chicagotribune.com/news/nationworld/ct-police-shootings-race-20160711-story.html.

82. Quoted in Martha Stoddard, "Trooper with KKK Link Is Back: His Due Process Rights and Contract Were Violated When He Was Fired, His Union Rep Says," *Omaha World-Herald*, August 27, 2006, p. B1.

83. Quoted in "Sanders to Gay-Bashers: 'You Are Cowards,'" Sign On San Diego, July 31, 2006. www.signonsandiego.com/news/metro/20060731-1532-hatecrime.html.

84. Quoted in Geoffrey Fattah, "Three Charged with Hate Crimes," *Salt Lake City Deseret Morning News*, November 4, 2005, p. B1.

Chapter 7: What Can People Do to Stop the Hate?

85. Quoted in Austin Fenner and Scott Shifrel, "Fat Nick Gets 15 Years," *New York Daily News*, July 18, 2006, p. 7.

86. Quoted in Anti-Defamation League, "How to Combat Bias and Hate Crimes: An ADL Blueprint for Action," 1999. www.adl.org/99hatecrime.

87. Quoted in Nancy Bartley, "An Act of Hate Brings Faiths Together," *Seattle Times*, August 1, 2006, p. A1.

88. Quoted in Bartley, "Act of Hate Brings Faiths Together," p. A1.

89. Carl Miller, "Social Media Is Driving the Rise of Hate Crime, but It Can also Stop It," *Telegraph*, October 12, 2015. www.telegraph.co.uk/news/uknews/crime/11925950/Social-media-is-driving-the-rise-of-hate-crime-but-it-can-also-stop-it.html.

90. Debra Chasnoff, "How to Stop Hate Crimes," *Advocate*, August 15, 2006. www.advocate.com/exclusive_detail_ektid35448.asp.

91. Quoted in Public Broadcasting Service, "Not In Our Town."

92. Quoted in KQED, "Not In Our Town, Northern California: Citizens Take Action." www.kqed.org/programs/tv/niot/coco.jsp.

93. Quoted in Hawley, "A Message of Tolerance, Peace," p. B1.

94. Quoted in Mike Cassego, "Remembering Matthew Shepard," *York (PA) Daily Record*, April 9, 2004, p. 1.

95. Quoted in Bullard, *Teaching Tolerance*, p. xix.

96. Michaelis, "This Is How You Become a White Supremacist."

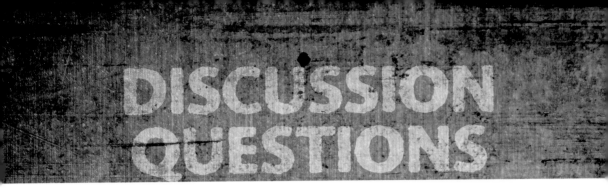

Chapter 1: Why Do People Hate?

1. Have you ever heard of an example of hate crimes, such as those discussed here?

2. How do stereotypes make it easier for people to hate other people?

3. Is the hatred some people feel for people who are different caused by fear?

Chapter 2: Hated for Their Race

1. Where does racial bias come from?

2. What impact do racist hate crimes have on individuals and communities?

3. How do historical events such as the Vietnam War make some people hate other people?

Chapter 3: Hated for Their Religion

1. Can you think of any examples of someone being made fun of for their religion?

2. Name some religious groups that are targeted for hate crimes. Who hates them?

3. Why do some people hate Muslims? Is it fair to blame all Muslims for actions by Muslim extremists?

Chapter 4: Hated for Their Sexual Orientation or Gender Identity

1. Which group of people targeted for hate crimes does Mark Potok of the Southern Poverty Law Center believe is hated more than any other?

2. Why are so many hate crimes against LGBT+ people never reported?

3. Are hate crimes a big problem in schools?

Chapter 5: Hated for Being Different

1. Have you or someone you know ever experienced prejudice because of being different?

2. Why might a hate-crime perpetrator mistake a Sikh for a Muslim?

3. Do you think there are any other groups who might experience hate crimes that have not been mentioned? Should there be hate crime laws protecting these groups?

Chapter 6: The Haters

1. Which is the oldest U.S. hate group? Is it still active in promoting hatred and committing hate crimes?

2. Do most people who commit hate crimes belong to hate groups?

3. Why do people join hate groups?

Chapter 7: What Can People Do to Stop the Hate?

1. If you were in charge, what kind of laws would you make to prevent hate crimes?

2. What part do groups play in fighting hate crime?

3. What can individual people do to stop hate crimes?

American Association of People with Disabilities
2013 H Street NW, 5th Floor
Washington, DC 20006
(800) 840-8844
www.aapd.com
This national association helps people cope with disabilities and fight discrimination and hate crimes.

Anti-Defamation League
(212) 885-7700
www.adl.org
One of the oldest groups in the United States that fights discrimination, the ADL battles hatred through educational and legal efforts.

Human Rights Campaign
1640 Rhode Island Avenue NW
Washington, DC 20036
(202) 628-4160
www.hrc.org
The Human Rights Campaign is the nation's largest civil rights organization working for LGBT+ equality.

National Association for the Advancement of Colored People
NAACP National Headquarters
4805 Mt. Hope Drive
Baltimore, MD 21215
(877) NAACP-98
www.naacp.org
The NAACP, a predominantly African American organization, has led the fight for black civil rights and to end discrimination since 1909.

National Coalition for the Homeless
2201 P Street NW
Washington, DC 20037
(202) 462-4822
www.nationalhomeless.org
The group works to protect homeless people from discrimination and hate crimes.

Southern Poverty Law Center
400 Washington Avenue
Montgomery, AL 36104
(888) 414-7752
www.splcenter.org
This organization was founded in 1971 to combat hate crimes and discrimination against Southern blacks. Today, it fights hate crimes and discrimination against all types of people.

Books

Barnes, Annie S. *Everyday Racism: A Book for All Americans.* Naperville, IL: Sourcebooks, 2000.
Barnes details various types of racism and hate crimes that people encounter at school, in the workplace, and in public places.

Citron, Danielle Keats. *Hate Crimes in Cyberspace.* Cambridge, MA: Harvard University Press, 2016.
As people's interactions increasingly take place online, society must broaden the definition of hate crimes to include incidents that take place on the Internet, which are detailed in this book.

Gitlin, Marty. *When Is Free Speech Hate Speech?* New York, NY: Greenhaven Publishing, 2017.
The Constitution protects freedom of speech, but just because people can say something does not mean they always should. This book offers some opinions on what is considered hate speech and whether or not it should be banned by the government.

Jelloun, Tahar Ben. *Racism Explained to My Daughter.* New York, NY: New Press, 2006.
Ben Jelloun and several other people discuss how they have explained racism to their children.

Stern-LaRosa, Caryl, and Ellen Hofheimer Bettmann. *The Anti-Defamation League's Hate Hurts: How Children Learn and Unlearn Prejudice.* New York, NY: Scholastic, 2000.
This book explores ways to keep children from becoming hateful and has advice on how to cope with hate.

Websites

Document Hate
documenthate.org
People can use this website to report when they have been the victim of a hate crime. The Document Hate project hopes to provide more accurate hate-crime statistics than the FBI, which does not collect all data from state and local law enforcement agencies.

Lambda Legal
www.lambdalegal.org
This website has detailed information on how to prevent, report, and survive hate crimes against LGBT+ people.

National Youth Violence Prevention Resource Center
www.safeyouth.org
This website, sponsored by several federal agencies, has information on how young people can prevent hate crimes.

Parents, Family, and Friends of Lesbians and Gays (PFLAG)
www.pflag.org
This organization supports LGBT+ people as well as their friends and family.

Partners Against Hate
www.partnersagainsthate.org
This is a national coalition of several groups that fight all types of hate crimes. Member groups include the Anti-Defamation League, the Leadership Conference Education Fund, and the Center for the Prevention of Hate Violence.

INDEX

Cover Abid Katib/Getty Images; p. 8 AP Photo/Susan Ragan; pp. 11, 49 Joe Raedle/Getty Images; p. 13 SolStock/E+/Getty Images; p. 15 NadzeyaShanchuk/Shutterstock.com; p. 19 Matt McClain/The Washington Post via Getty Images; p. 23 (map) vasosh/iStock/Thinkstock; p. 25 Gilles Petard/Redferns/Getty Images; p. 27 Topical Press Agency/Getty Images; p. 31 Bettmann/Contributor/Bettmann/Getty Images; p. 34 Ariel Skelley/ Photographer's Choice/Getty Images; p. 37 1000 Words/ Shutterstock.com; p. 39 Everett Historical/Shutterstock.com; p. 42 Arindam Shivaani/NurPhoto via Getty Images; p. 45 DAVID HANCOCK/AFP/Getty Images; p. 46 National Archive/Newsmakers/Getty Images; p. 55 VWPics/ Alamy Stock Photo; p. 56 Getty Images/Handout/Hulton Archive/Getty Images; p. 59 Rocketclips, Inc./Shutterstock.com; p. 62 Joseph Sohm/ Shutterstock.com; p. 64 kali9/E+/Getty Images; p. 68 juefraphoto/iStock/ Thinkstock; p. 70 AP Photo/Morry Gash; p. 72 William Thomas Cain/Getty Images; p. 74 Sean Gallup/Getty Images; p. 77 Markus Matzel/ullstein bild via Getty Images; p. 79 Andrew Burton/Getty Images; p. 81 Afro American Newspapers/Gado/Getty Images; p. 84 Chris Ryan/OJO Images/Getty Images; p. 87 Rawpixel.com/Shutterstock.com; p. 90 Carlos Osorio/Toronto Star via Getty Images; p. 92 Neilson Barnard/Getty Images for Logo.

ABOUT THE AUTHOR

Meghan Sharif is a writer and avid reader. When her nose is not in a book, she works as a full-time teacher for adults with disabilities. In her free time, she enjoys yoga, crocheting, and kickboxing. She lives in Central Pennsylvania.